ABOUT THE AUTHOR

After studying Modern History at Durham University,
Graham Berry taught and examined History for many
years. Although he has contributed to educational text
books, *Aftermath* is his first book written for the general
public. The author lives in Richmond, North Yorkshire.

To Mike

Enjoy the walk! Best
wishes.

Graham Berry

DEDICATION

I would like to dedicate the book to my two
granddaughters, Olivia and Isabel. I hope that they will
come to share my own love of History.

Graham Berry

AFTERMATH

1918-24:
Years that Shaped the Twentieth Century

AUSTIN MACAULEY PUBLISHERS™

LONDON • CAMBRIDGE • NEW YORK • SHARJAH

A CIP catalogue record for this title is available from the British Library.

ISBN 978-1-78693-737-7 (Paperback)
ISBN 978-1-78693-738-4 (E-Book)
www.austinmacauley.com

First Published (2017)
Austin Macauley Publishers™ Ltd.
25 Canada Square
Canary Wharf
London
E14 5LQ

ACKNOWLEDGEMENTS

I would like to thank my brother Melvyn and my friends Bob and Mary Wallace and Moira Smith for finding the time to read and comment on my draft chapters. A special acknowledgement goes to my fellow Historian, Elizabeth Sparey, for her many helpful suggestions and points of detail. Whilst acknowledging their help, any shortcomings in the text remain very much my own.

CONTENTS

Author's Note

MAJOR WARS ARE A CATALYST FOR CHANGE. THE History of the twentieth century and recent events in the Middle East have shown that wars often have significant and long-lasting effects. Only the perspective of time allows us to fully assess their significance. As we move towards the centenary of the ending of the Great War in November 1918, it would seem appropriate, therefore, to consider the aftermath of World War 1, the first 'world war'.

Through a series of overlapping chapters, *Aftermath* seeks to build up an understanding of the influence of World War 1 on the actions and events of the years 1918 to 1924 and how they, in turn, helped to shape the twentieth century. The aftermath of World War 1 shaped not just the development of the defeated Central Powers in the years after 1918 but, also, that of the victorious allies. In different ways, for example, Britain was just as affected by its involvement in World War 1 as was Germany. Each chapter explores different aspects of these effects, from the impact of the Treaty of Versailles on Germany to the emergence of 'Modern Britain'.

In many respects, from the effects of the collapse of the Ottoman Empire in the Middle East to the division of Ireland, we are still experiencing the impact of the actions and events which took place in the aftermath of World War 1.

Each of the chapters merits a detailed study of its own. 'Aftermath' is, by intent, a broad survey of these different aspects. Even the series of chapters on 'Britain' is limited to a focus mainly on England and Ireland. There is, therefore, scope for the reader to explore further. The following offer a few suggestions for further reading.

Hundred Days: The End of the Great War: Nick Lloyd (2013)

The 1918 Spanish Flu Pandemic: The History and Legacy of the World's Deadliest Influenza Outbreak: Charles Rivers Editors (2017)

Paris 1919: Six Months that Changed the World: Margaret MacMillan (2003)

A Line in the Sand: Britain, France and the struggle that shaped the Middle East: James Barr (2012)

A People's Tragedy: Orlando Figes (2017)

Anxious Decades: America in Prosperity and Depression 1920-1941: Michael E. Parrish (1994)

The Making of Modern Britain: From Queen Victoria to VE Day: Andrew Marr (2010)

Ireland in the 20th Century: Tim Pat Coogan (2004)

CHAPTER 1
Peace: the end of War in Europe

EVER SINCE THE GERMAN ADVANCE INTO NORTH-
ern France was halted at the Battle of the Marne in September 1914, the Western Front had witnessed a bloody stalemate. World War 1, which had begun as a war of rapid
movement, had become a war of attrition, with a line of
heavily defended trenches, protected by barbed wire and
machine guns, stretching from the English Channel to the
Swiss border.

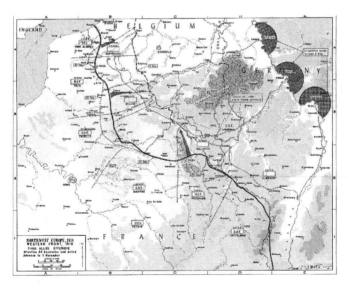

The line of trenches during the First World War

13

The Battle of Passchendaele, 1917

Despite great pitched battles such as the Somme 1916 and Passchendaele 1917, four years of bloodshed and mud had brought no decisive breakthrough. The sacrifice of the ordinary soldiers on both sides seemed to have been in vain as their generals continued to pursue a strategy of wearing down the enemy and breaking through their lines in one great push. 'Lions led by donkeys' is a term popularly used to describe the heroics of the ordinary British soldier and the lack of imagination or flexibility in tactics of their leaders, such as the commander-in-chief, Field Marshal Sir Douglas Haig.

Douglas Haig was promoted to command the British First Army in 1915. In December of that same year he became British commander-in-chief. Haig is particularly associated with the casualties and failures of the great set-piece battles such as the Somme 1916 and the Third Battle of Ypres 1917, known as Passchendaele. He is less well known today for his leadership of the sweeping military successes of the '100 Days' in the summer and autumn of 1918 which saw him end the war as a national hero.

At the start of 1918 a breakthrough to end the stalemate of the Western Front seemed as far away as ever. The German forces were strongly entrenched behind their 'Siegfriedstellung' or Hindenburg Line as it was called by the British, a series of strong defensive points occupied since the spring of 1917. Though some breaches of the Line had been made by Britain and her allies, such as at Cambrai in November 1917, it remained largely intact and was considered by the Germans to be impregnable. As a new year dawned, there was little to suggest that victory was near. The German position had even been strengthened by the Bolshevik (Communist) Revolution in Russia in November 1917. Promising 'Peace, Bread and Land' and intent on first consolidating the revolution within Russia, Lenin, the Bolshevik leader, signed the humiliating Treaty of Brest-Litovsk with Germany in March 1918. The freeing up of German forces from the Eastern Front then allowed Hindenburg to launch his Spring Offensives against Britain and her allies on the Western Front.

Field Marshal Sir Douglas Haig

The defences of the Hindenburg Line

After his success in defeating the Russian army at Tannenberg in 1914, Hindenburg became commander of German forces on the Eastern Front. In August 1916 he was made supreme commander of German forces. Aided by his chief of staff, Major-General Ludendorff, Hindenburg largely shaped Germany's strategy for the rest of the war. His strategy for the Western Front was to strengthen German defences by building the Hindenburg Line. Despite the failure of the Spring Offensives of 1918, Hindenburg remained in command of the German Army until July 1919 and served as President of the Weimar Republic from 1924 until 1934.

After four years of stalemate, 1918 saw the transformation of the fortunes of Britain and her allies on the Western Front. It was to be the year of the long hoped for breakthrough as the war of attrition turned back to a war of movement. Military and political events began to unfold with increasing speed. The rapidity with which the logjam of the Western Front began to be dismantled in the

16

summer and autumn of 1918 has raised many questions for historians.

Left to right: Field Marshal Paul von Hindenburg, Kaiser Wilhelm II, Major-General Ludendorff

Was it mainly caused by the arrival of fresh troops and resources from the USA? Was it caused by Hindenburg's decision (influenced by the collapse of Russia and by the entry of the USA into the war) to launch a series of great offensives in the spring of 1918 rather than to continue to defend behind his Siegfriedstellung? Had the much maligned British and French generals learnt from the years of bloodshed and stalemate to develop new tactics? Did the war end because the unfolding events on the Western Front shaped political developments in Germany, bringing about a new political regime and the decision to surrender? Was the German army truly defeated or, as was later claimed by nationalists such as Hitler, was it stabbed in the back by the 'November criminals' of the Weimar government?

17

The USA had been close to declaring war on Germany in May 1915 when the Cunard liner, RMS Lusitania, had been sunk by a German U-Boat off the coast of Ireland, resulting in the loss of 128 American citizens. President Wilson described it as an 'unlawful and inhumane act' and warned that the USA would regard any subsequent attacks that caused the loss of American lives as 'deliberately unfriendly'. Fearing American entry into the conflict, Germany had halted its policy of unrestricted U-Boat warfare (the sinking of merchant ships by submarines in international waters without warning). In the spring of 1917, however, Germany took the calculated gamble to resume the policy.

The decision was taken because of the German unwillingness to once again risk its High Seas Fleet in battle against the British Grand Fleet after the naval engagement at Jutland in May 1916. Although the British Grand Fleet had lost more ships than the Germans in the Battle of Jutland (the only major naval engagement between the German High Seas Fleet and the British Grand Fleet during WW1), the battle convinced Admiral Scheer, the German commander, that a fleet action could not win the war for Germany. For the remainder of the war, the German High Seas Fleet remained in its naval bases around the North Sea and the Baltic, such as Wilhelmshaven and Kiel. The High Seas Fleet was eventually to surrender to the British soon after the ending of WW1 in November 1918. In one last act of defiance, the ships were then scuttled at Scapa Flow in Orkney in June 1919 by their German skeleton crews to prevent the ships from being seized by the allied powers. Most of the ships remain there today, a popular destination for divers.

Despite a clear warning from President Wilson that the sinking of American ships would lead to the USA joining the war on the side of Britain and her allies, Admiral Scheer and others convinced the Kaiser in 1917 that, with its High Seas Fleet unable to win the war, Germany should resume unrestricted U-boat warfare. The Germans hoped that they could sink enough ships to starve Britain into surrender before the entry of the USA into the war could have a decisive effect. It was to prove a gamble that failed.

Engraving of German U-boat from The Illustrated London News

The decision to resume unrestricted U-boat warfare came soon after the infamous 'Zimmerman Telegram', a message sent by the German Foreign Secretary, Arthur Zimmerman, to the German ambassador in Mexico in January 1917. The telegram, which offered German assistance to Mexico to regain its 'lost' territories of Texas, Arizona and New Mexico in the event of a war between Germany and the USA, had been picked up by British naval intelligence and passed to the Americans. Together with Germany's resumption of unrestricted U-Boat warfare, the revelation of the Zimmerman Telegram meant that the pressure on the USA to act became unstoppable.

In April 1917, the USA declared war on Germany and her allies.

American soldiers in action

The entry of the USA into World War 1 inevitably began to tip the balance in favour of Britain and her allies in terms of resources, so contributing to the breaking of the stalemate. Although the USA lacked a large standing army, her mobilization was rapid. The commander of the American Expeditionary Force (AEF) was General John Pershing. By May 1918 there were more than half a million American troops in France and, by the time of the great Allied offensives of July 1918, that figure had risen to over a million. When the war ended in November 1918, American forces comprised one-third of the total Allied force.

Field Marshal von Hindenburg was later to state that 'Without the American troops and despite a food blockade … the war could have ended in a stalemate.'

The arrival of so many fresh troops to share the burden of warfare on the Western Front changed the whole mindset and morale of the Allies.

From the time of their first engagement with the Germans in May 1918 at Cantigny, American forces took part in some fierce fighting. American success at Cantigny did much to raise the morale of Britain and her allies as their forces buckled under the weight of the German offensives. American troops fought alongside French and British forces at the second battle of the Marne in July 1918 that once again stopped the German advance on Paris. Bloodiest of all was the Battle of Meuse-Argonne in September 1918. More than one million American soldiers assaulted the German lines, with their commander, General Pershing, believing that the superiority of American 'guts' over machine guns, barbed wire, massed artillery and poison gas would win the day. His claim that, in 36 hours, the Doughboys would crack open German defences and clear the road to

Berlin, was naively reminiscent of claims made by British and French commanders earlier in the war. Years of bloody attrition and stalemate had since taught them differently. The USA quickly learned the lesson for itself. Among the ranks of the American soldiers fighting at Meuse-Argonne were the future President, Harry S. Truman, the future Second World War generals, Patton and MacArthur, and George Marshall, the architect of the Marshall Plan (the American plan for re-building Europe after the devastation of WW2). It was to prove the bloodiest battle the USA had ever fought, with more than 120,000 casualties, including 26,000 dead, although today it is largely forgotten in the USA.

Perhaps most crucial was the effect that the entry of the USA into the war had on German strategy. The prospect of large numbers of American troops arriving in France made Ludendorff and Hindenburg decide to abandon their defensive strategy and launch a series of major offensives in the spring of 1918. The calculation was that the Americans would not be able to make a decisive impact until the early summer. The Bolshevik Revolution and Russia's withdrawal from the war at Brest-Litovsk, signed in March 1918, allowed the Germans to withdraw troops from the Eastern Front to strengthen their forces in the West. Though not as many troops as hoped for were able to be released, the increased numbers were bolstered by new German tactics. Each division was given additional mortars and machine guns to increase their firepower. Elite formations of storm troopers were formed to lead attacks and to exploit the paralyzing effect of intense bombardments of the enemy rear lines preceding any attack.

The initial focus was to be on the British lines between Arras and St Quentin in an attempt to separate the British forces from the French and roll them back to the Channel. It was a great strategic gamble and was to prove to be Germany's last throw of the dice. Its failure was to prove decisive to Germany's military defeat on the Western Front.

German soldiers

The first offensive, Operation Michael, began in March 1918. The shock of the intense bombardment on the over-stretched and poorly co-ordinated defences of the British lines was devastating. As German storm troopers began to attack, the British were forced to pull back. As the offensives continued and spread, so the Allies were forced to withdraw further. On 10 April, with the situation deteriorating, Haig issued his famous Order of the Day that, 'Every position must be held to the last man. There must be no retirement. With our backs to the wall and believing in the justice of our cause, each one must fight on to the end. The safety of our homes and the freedom of mankind alike depend upon the conduct of each one of us at this critical moment.'

Critically, however, the line did not break, even though it buckled and withdrew. The appointment of Ferdinand Foch as supreme commander over Haig in April 1918 saw a decisive response, with French troops pouring in to plug the gaps.

Marshal Foch was associated with a belief in offensive warfare. As commander of the French Ninth Army in 1914 he had successfully led the counterattack at the Battle of the Marne that had stopped the German advance through France. Side-lined for political reasons after the Battle of the Somme 1916, he was recalled by Petain in 1917 as Chief of the General Staff. He became the Allied commander-in-chief in April 1918, working closely with Haig on their offensives that summer. Foch was created a Marshal of France in August 1918 after the Second Battle of the Marne.

Marshal Ferdinand Foch (left) with General Pershing

The ability of Britain, France and their allies to resist German offensives without breaking began to demoralize and to frustrate Ludendorff. With ever more American troops flooding in, the Germans made one last effort to break through with an assault on the French held Chemin des Dames on 27 May. The German breakthrough advanced as far as the Marne, just as it had in the first advances of 1914 through northern France. With Paris once again ahead of them, however, the Spring Offensives ran out of momentum and resources. The Allies, aided by freshly arrived American troops, began to counter-attack, and Ludendorff ordered his men to a halt. The Second Battle of the Marne was to prove the beginning of the end for the German army on the Western Front. For the loss of one million casualties, Ludendorff had exhausted German's military resources without gaining any decisive breakthrough. The stage was set for the Allied counter-offensives of 1918, the so-called '100 Days'.

The foundations for the sweeping Allied victories of the summer and autumn of 1918 had been laid down in 1917, with the development of new technology and fighting methods. German dominance of the air had gradually been negated by the sheer number of Allied aircraft. New tactics and roles for aircraft had been developed such as close air support for advancing troops to disrupt enemy defences. On 1 April 1918 the Royal Flying Corps became the Royal Air Force (RAF) with the intention of fully integrating air power into the imminent offensives.

Of even greater significance had been the first use of massed tanks as an offensive weapon at Cambrai in November 1917 on part of the 'impregnable' Hindenburg Line. This was combined with 'silent registration' – the ability of artillery to open up directly onto the front lines of enemy trenches without 'ranging fire' that had both warned the enemy of an imminent attack and churned up the ground in front of the enemy. Instead of firing shells for days beforehand to break up the enemy barbed wire, this task would now be achieved by the tanks. The artillery would open up suddenly at 'zero hour' to destroy German trenches in a series of 'creeping barrages', destroying one line of trenches and then the ones behind.

Tanks at Nanteuil la Fosse, northern France, 1917

Combining close air support, massed tanks and silent registration of artillery, the British had both surprised and shocked the German troops at Cambrai. The tanks were able to roll through what the Germans had considered to be impregnable barbed wire and cross over trenches that were deemed too deep and too wide for artillery to surmount. Though the attack ran out of steam and failed to achieve the hoped-for breakthrough, Cambrai had shown that the tactics of combining artillery, tanks and infantry in a new way did have the potential to break through. The problem was how to sustain initial successes. The lessons learned were to be fully exploited in the summer of 1918.

Central to the Allied achievements and successes in the '100 Days' was their overwhelming advantage in aircraft, artillery, tanks and infantry weapons by 1918. This contrasted sharply with the exhaustion of Germany's troops and resources.

'Our lines are falling back. There are too many
fresh English and American regiments out there ...
Too many new guns. Too many aeroplanes ... Our
artillery is fired out, it has too few shells ... Our
fresh troops are anaemic boys in need of rest, who
cannot carry a pack, but merely know how to die.
By thousands ...'

Erich Maria Remarque, *All Quiet on the Western Front*

The Allied offensives of the '100 Days' began with the Battle
of Amiens on 8 August 1918. Exploiting the use of silent
registration of artillery, 530 tanks and air attacks, co-ordinated to an unprecedented extent by the use of radio
communication, the British made major gains. Ludendorff
described 8 August as the, 'Black day of the German army
in the history of the war.' By the middle of September the
Allied forces had reached as far as the Hindenburg Line. In
a series of sweeping offensives their forces breached the
whole line, including a crossing of the St Quentin canal,
and broke through into open countryside.

The Allied counter-offensive that brought World War 1
to an end was spearheaded by the British army under Field
Marshal Haig. Widely criticised for his association with
the inflexible and futile set-piece battles earlier in the war,
such as the Somme and Passchendaele, Haig was able to
exploit overwhelming Allied resources by the late summer
of 1918 and to master the complex developments in tactics
and technology that had evolved since 1914. Despite being
under the overall command of Foch from April 1918,
Haig's leadership of the sweeping military successes of the
'100 Days' saw him end the war as a national hero and one
of the most successful British generals ever. Haig's funeral

in 1928 was declared a day of national mourning and was a huge state occasion.

It was to be the publication of Lloyd George's *War Memoirs* between 1933 and 1938 that began the weakening of Haig's reputation. Lloyd George claimed that the driving force behind the Allied victories in the summer and autumn of 1918 was not Haig but Marshal Foch. He blamed Haig's inflexible tactics for the 'massacre of brave men', often for limited gains, as during the Somme offensive. Lloyd George accused Haig of sticking rigidly to his outdated plans for hurling millions of shells and hundreds of thousands of men at German strongpoints. The dynamism of the '100 Days', claimed Lloyd George, came not from Haig but from Foch. In a damning put-down, Lloyd George described Haig as 'brilliant to the top of his army boots'.

Lloyd George's dismissal of Haig's achievements by 1918 was based, in part, on the fact that the two men had clashed repeatedly throughout the war about military tactics and both had built up a sense of resentment towards the other. A new edition of Haig's wartime diaries and letters, edited by Gary Sheffield and John Bourne, reveal how Haig, exasperated by Lloyd George, repeatedly confided in King George V. In doing so, he stretched constitutional convention to the limit and added to the conflict between the two war leaders. Lloyd George's *War Memoirs* were designed to 'set the record straight' as to his own part in winning the war. With Cabinet papers from the war period sealed until the 1960s, it was Lloyd George's views that, for many years, served as the main basis for interpreting Haig's role during World War 1.

As their army began to disintegrate on the Western Front, so Germany had been collapsing from within during the course of 1918. Both external and internal factors were integral to bringing about her surrender. Ever since the outbreak of war, the Royal Navy had been able to enforce an effective blockade of German ports, preventing any vessels from either entering or leaving. The return of the German High Seas Fleet to its naval bases after the Battle of Jutland ensured that the blockade continued throughout the war. By 1918 the blockade was causing not just a lack of raw materials for military production but also grave food shortages and social unrest. The failure of the German Spring Offensives and the Allied advances in the '100 Days' disillusioned and demoralized many in Germany, causing a loss of faith in the Imperial government. Political unrest grew and became more radical and outspoken. Of particular concern was the growing call for a Bolshevik revolution, inspired by the Russian Revolution of the previous November. A German communist party, the Spartacist League led by Karl Liebknecht and Rosa Luxembourg, began to agitate for revolution and a workers' government.

The Kaiser responded to the growing unrest by offering a constitutional monarchy and to make the government answerable to an elected parliament. His offer was too little, too late. The situation within Germany was spiralling out of control. In early November 1918 the sailors at Kiel mutinied, refusing the order to put to sea for a final sortie that would save the honor of the German Navy. The mutineers began to call for revolution and the Kaiser's brother had to flee the city in disguise. As the Allied advances continued on the Western Front, General Ludendorff wanted to continue the war. His views, however, were at odds with the growing crisis within Germany. Amid fears that the country might explode into revolution if made to fight on, Ludendorff resigned on 26 October. His parting words were to prove prophetic: 'In a fortnight we shall have no Empire and no Emperor left, you will see.'

The Kiel Uprising, November 1918

His military successor, Wilhelm Groener, warned the Kaiser that the army could not be relied upon to put down the revolutionaries. Ebert, the leader of the majority Social Democrat Party, warned that, 'The Kaiser must abdicate, otherwise we shall have the revolution.' Dissuaded from his notion that the army could be turned against the revolutionaries within Germany and with little alternative left to him, on 9 November Kaiser Wilhelm abdicated and fled to the Netherlands, where his first request was to ask for a 'cup of good English tea'.

Germany became a republic, headed by its Chancellor Fritz Ebert, though he did not become President until February 1919 when the Weimar Republic was proclaimed. Negotiations for an armistice had already begun two days earlier, when a German delegation crossed Allied lines to begin discussions with the French. These were concluded in a railway carriage in the Forest of Compiègne. At 11.00 a.m. on 11 November 1918 the guns finally fell silent.

The signing of the Armistice

With no Allied soldiers on German soil and the surrender being announced so soon after the coming to power of Ebert and the Social Democrats, many Germans did not understand the reality of the stark military position facing their country. Returning German soldiers were fêted as heroes. Encouraged by the post-war writing of General Ludendorff, who claimed that he had only been deprived of victory by sinister forces operating behind the scenes, the myth developed of the 'stab in the back' by the 'November criminals', the politicians who had signed the armistice and agreed to the humiliating Treaty of Versailles. Even though the politicians had had no choice, this myth was to be exploited by Hitler and the Nazis to undermine the Weimar Republic.

CHAPTER 2
The Spanish Flu 1918–19:
a forgotten pandemic

AS WORLD WAR 1 MOVED TOWARDS ITS CLOSE
with the unfolding events of 1918, so a new cause of
death began to emerge, one that was even more deadly
and widespread than the war. This was the Spanish Flu
pandemic of 1918 to 1919. (The term 'pandemic' is applied
to a wide-scale and rapidly spreading epidemic). It affected
approximately 500 million people, one third of the world's
population. It spread right around the globe, including
remote Pacific islands and the Arctic. With a death rate
between 10 and 20%, five to twenty times that expected
of a 'normal' flu pandemic, it is estimated to have killed
at least 50 million people worldwide. This was approximately three to five percent of the world's population and
more than three times the death toll of World War 1. In the
USA alone, 28% of the population caught the Spanish Flu,
with between 500,000 and 675,000 casualties. In Britain,
as many as 250,000 died. One of the worst affected places
was Western Samoa, where 90% of the population was
affected, killing 30% of the adult men and 22% of the
adult women. All levels of society were affected. In Spain,
King Alfonso XIII was one of the victims. President Wilson
of the USA survived the flu virus, as did the British Prime

Minister David Lloyd George and Winston Churchill's wife and daughter, though their nanny died from it.

Even more unusual was the demographic range worst hit by the Spanish Flu pandemic. Normal flu epidemics mostly affect the very young and very old or those whose health is poor. In the case of the Spanish Flu pandemic of 1918 to 1919, the worst hit were fit and healthy adults in the age range of 20 to 40. In the USA, 99% of the deaths were of people under the age of 65.

The Spanish Flu pandemic of 1918 to 1919 was the greatest medical holocaust in history. It killed more people in one year than the Black Death killed in the entire 14th century. It killed more people in 24 weeks than AIDS has killed in 24 years. It targeted the fit and healthy in the prime of their lives. Yet it remains the 'forgotten pandemic', overtaken in public awareness by modern pandemics such as AIDS. Even today, it remains shrouded in elements of uncertainty as to why it came in three waves, what its exact cause was and why it killed so many people, especially those not normally susceptible to death from flu epidemics.

Though the Spanish Flu pandemic came in three waves, the gap between the waves was brief and, in some places, hard to discern. Its exact origins are unclear. It was first observed in the USA in Haskell County, Kansas, in January 1918. On 4 March a company cook, Albert Mitchell, reported sick at Fort Riley, Kansas. By noon on 18 March more than 100 soldiers were in hospital. Numbers quickly rose in the days that followed and the virus spread rapidly outwards. This first wave was more like a normal flu epidemic.

Doctors even called it the 'three day fever'. Troops in the trenches adopted the French name for it, 'la grippe'. A second, much more deadly wave, spread globally between

September and November 1918. In many nations, a third wave occurred in January 1919. It is not even clear whether the three waves were the same virus or whether it mutated over an unusually short time frame. What was clear was that those who had caught and survived the first, less lethal, outbreak seemed to have some immunity to the more deadly second wave. Even the timing of the waves was unusual. Influenza is normally most prevalent in winter. The Spanish Flu was at its most deadly in the autumn.

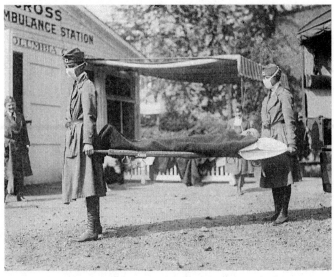

Red Cross litter carriers during Spanish Flu pandemic

Then, as suddenly as it had appeared, the deadly Spanish Flu seemed to have mutated and passed into history. It became known as the 'Spanish Flu' only because the authorities in Germany, France, Britain and the USA imposed a strict censorship to play down fears over the rapid spread and mortality rate of the disease lest it cause panic. Spain was neutral and did not have the same level of censorship, so the severe outbreak of the disease there was more widely reported. It seemed to other countries, ignorant of their own outbreaks, that Spain was especially hard hit. In popular minds the disease became associated with Spain, hence the 'Spanish Flu' or the 'Spanish Lady'. In Spain itself, the disease was called 'the Naples Soldier' because an opera singer had joked that the disease was as catching as a popular song entitled 'the Naples Soldier'.

Various theories have been put forward to try and explain the origins of the Spanish Flu and its high mortality rate among adults in the age range 20 to 40. In 1997 samples of the virus were collected from the remains of a female flu victim. She had died in a tiny Alaskan town called Braving Mission, where 85% of the population had been hit by the flu in one week. Her body had been preserved in the Alaskan permafrost. Samples had also been preserved from the bodies of American soldiers who died of the flu. These samples have been used to try and determine the origins of the pandemic. In 2005 it was announced that the virus's genetic sequence had been determined. It was a variant of the classic H1N1 influenza virus that had evolved from an avian strain and developed the ability to jump to humans. In 2014 scientists in the USA controversially recreated the 1918 virus from fragments of avian flu found in wild ducks. The virus they recreated is 97% identical to those recovered from the frozen corpse. The structure of the virus's protein coat had developed, so enabling it to bond with receptors on human cells deep within the lungs. Despite attempts to link its origins to different parts of the globe, such as China, there is still no conclusive evidence as to how and where it evolved into the deadly strain of the Spanish Flu. There is a theory that it had been circulating around the world for some years before mutating into the pandemic virus of 1918. What is clear is that the 1918 strain exclusively affected humans.

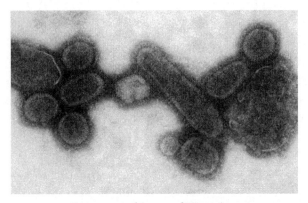

Reconstructed image of H1 antigen

One theory about the unusual mortality distribution has been that older people may have gained some immunity from the 'Russian' flu epidemic of 1889-90. Unfortunately, there is no medical trace of this precursor virus. A more recent theory is that the virus triggered an overreaction in the body's immune system. This would explain why deaths were highest in young adults, who would have had a strong immune system, and lower in the elderly and young, whose immune systems would have been weaker.

Death from the Spanish Flu was particularly gruesome. Within hours of feeling the first flu-like symptoms – headaches, fatigue and fever – those affected began to turn blue from a lack of oxygen. Patients began to cough violently, some with such force that they tore their abdominal muscles. Many died from secondary pneumonia infections, but others were killed directly by massive hemorrhages and oedema in the lungs. There were reports of patients 'struggling to clear their airways of blood-tinged froth that sometimes gushed from their nose and mouth.' (Isaac Starr, *Influenza in 1918: Recollections of the Epidemic in Philadelphia*). A navy nurse, Josie Brown, who was stationed at Great Lakes Naval Station near Chicago, described how, 'They would have terrific nosebleeds with it. Sometimes the blood would just shoot across the room. You had to get out of the way or someone's nose would bleed all over you'.

It was not until the 1940s that the first effective flu vaccine was developed. With no clearly proven method of prevention or treatment, even medical advice was contradictory. On the one hand, doctors advised rejecting all alcohol. Conversely, they recommended taking regular tots of whisky. Tobacco was thought to exacerbate the illness and was discouraged. Oxo spent large sums of money advertising their meat drink supplement as a way of 'fortifying the system'. *The News of the World* suggested washing inside your nose with soap and water each night and morning, forcing yourself to sneeze regularly, regular sharp walks and eating plenty of porridge! With no NHS system, many could not afford to pay for a doctor and simply relied on traditional cures, such as rhubarb, treacle and vinegar or gurgling with salt water. The principal advice seemed to be to stay in bed until the fever had passed and, above all, to keep children away from sick patients. As with the spread of the Black Death in the Middle Ages, the only certain way of avoiding the flu epidemic was isolation. In Alaska, a village just 30 miles from Braving Mission stationed armed guards at the perimeter to prevent anyone from entering. The village survived unscathed.

What is not in doubt is that World War 1 was a major factor in helping to spread the flu pandemic. The concentration and movement of troops in the war helped the spread of the disease among the very age range most at risk. Soldiers were crowded together in training camps. In the USA, the epidemic spread from Fort Riley camp to other training camps. One of the doctors at Camp Deveins in the U.S. wrote that, 'For several days there were no coffins and the bodies piled up something fierce: we used to go down to the morgue and look at the boys laid out in long rows. It beats any sight they ever had in France after a battle.' From the training camps, soldiers were crowded onto troop trains or, as with American soldiers, onto ships to be transported to Europe. It was American soldiers who brought the Spanish Flu to Europe. When they became ill, the worst affected soldiers were then sent to overcrowded military hospitals, such as that at Etaples, a major troop staging and hospital camp which was a centre for the second wave in France. It is estimated that, of the American soldiers who died in World War 1, more than half died of the Spanish Flu. Soldiers returning home from the Western Front helped to spread the flu to their home towns and cities. Just when the second wave seemed to be beginning to die away, the Armistice celebrations, in which huge crowds hugged and kissed each other, helped to re-launch it.

The everyday life of civilians was also severely affected while the epidemic was at its height. In the USA, gauze masks were issued to be worn in public. Stores could not hold sales. Funerals were to be limited to 15 minutes or, as was the case in Chicago for a time, banned altogether.

Railroads and some towns would not accept people without a signed certificate or if they were not wearing a mask. The New York Health Commissioner ordered businesses to open and close at staggered times so that there would be less crowding on the subway. Some of the British responses were typical of English sang-froid. The Savoy announced that it was in the grip of the 'Big Sneeze' and the barman invented a new cocktail, called a Corpse Reviver.

Bodies piled up as the epidemic spread. There was a shortage of both coffins and doctors, with many of the latter away at the war or affected themselves by the influenza. Medical Schools released third and fourth year students to help in the wards. In many places, mass graves had to be dug, reminiscent of the Black Death in the 14th century. In London, 1,500 policemen, a third of the force, reported sick simultaneously. Railway workshops in England turned to coffin manufacture and Red Cross ambulances became hearses. Social history is often reflected in children's nursery rhymes. One popular rhyme being sung in 1918 was as follows: I had a little bird; its name was Enza; I opened the window; and in-flew-Enza.

Given the scale and mortality rate of the pandemic it is surprising that it soon faded from public memory. This is partly because the outbreak was overshadowed by the events of World War 1. The media focus was more on the war than on the Spanish Flu. Certainly, in Britain, stories of the new epidemic were buried deep within the newspapers. A large number of young men were also being killed in the war and so the media reports merged the two causes of death in the popular mind, meaning that it had less of a psychological impact. Many simply wanted to put the horrors of the past behind them, both the war and the flu, and move forward in their lives. It also had a relatively short duration in any one area, compared to the four years that World War 1 lasted. After the deadly second wave, new cases dropped abruptly and, in many places, virtually disappeared. In Philadelphia, for example, 4,597 people died from the flu in the week beginning 16 October. By 11 November, the flu had almost disappeared from the city. This compares to the decades and even centuries of other diseases such as the Black Death in the Middle Ages and the intense media focus on more recent diseases such as AIDS. The Spanish Flu soon became the 'forgotten pandemic'.

There have been several flu pandemics since the Spanish Flu. The Asian Flu pandemic of 1957 to 1958 killed around two million people worldwide. The Hong Kong Flu pandemic of 1968 to 1969 killed approximately one million. In 2009 a variant of the 1918 H1N1 virus reappeared in Mexico. It became known as swine flu because the re-assortment of bird and human flu viruses was combined with two pig viruses. Estimates of the mortality toll for the 2009 to 2010 pandemic are hard to verify, with most deaths occurring in Africa and South-East Asia. Estimates vary from the World Health Organization figure of 284,500 to upwards of 579,000. Influenza remains a deadly killer, with periodic mutations of viruses that have a high mortality rate until the population gains immunity, whether from vaccination or herd immunity. Fortunately, none, so far, have gained the ability of the Spanish Flu pandemic to jump so rapidly from person to person and to kill with such deadly effect.

CHAPTER 3
The Treaty of Versailles:
a compromise that satisfied nobody

ON 18 JANUARY 1919 DELEGATES OF THE VICTO-
rious Allied powers assembled in Paris to begin the negotiations that would decide not just the punishments to be
imposed on the defeated powers but, also, to re-draw the
maps of Europe, Africa and the Middle East. Their decisions regarding Germany were signed in the Hall of Mirrors
at Versailles on 28 June 1919, exactly five years after
Gavrilo Princip had assassinated Archduke Franz

Signing the Treaty of Versailles in the Hall of Mirrors,
28 June 1919

Ferdinand of Austria and so begun the chain of events that had led to the outbreak of World War 1. For this reason, the settlement became known as the Treaty of Versailles. Separate treaties were to be signed with the other defeated powers.

The background against which they met and made these decisions was unprecedented. The world had been changed irrevocably by the pressures of the very first 'world war' and much of it was in a state of flux. In Russia the Tsar had fallen and a civil war was taking place. The Empires of Austria-Hungary and Turkey had collapsed. That of Germany was at the disposal of the Allies. Britain and France had themselves been exhausted by the demands of waging war. Belgium and northern France had suffered the devastation caused by a war of attrition fought on their soil. With its economy and trade benefiting from the war, the USA had emerged by 1918 as the wealthiest country in the world.

The Great War of 1914-18 was meant to be the 'war to end all wars'. No sooner had the Treaty of Versailles been signed, however, than commentators such as John Maynard Keynes, *The Economic Consequences of the Peace* (1919), were predicting that, rather than avert future conflict, the decisions made in Paris would actually cause future tensions and disputes. The outbreak of World War 2 has since been linked to the legacy of Versailles.

It is possible that such an outcome was inevitable. It was not just that the peace negotiators had to wrestle with complex and major issues. Their decisions were also influenced by who was there and who was not there. The defeated nations, Germany, Austria, Hungary and Turkey, were excluded from the discussions. The treaties were to be presented to them as a 'fait accompli'. Refusal to sign would bring the prospect of the armistice being rescinded and hostilities being resumed. This in itself was a cause of future German challenges to the terms imposed on them by the 'Diktat' of Versailles.

The negotiations began in chaos, swamped by more than one thousand statesmen, diplomats and officials discussing myriad topics in endless meetings with little overall structure. The British junior diplomat, Harold Nicholson, who later published *Peace-making 1919*, described it as 'a riot in a parrot-house'. To try and make some progress, key decisions began to be thrashed out by the lead delegates of the 'Big Four': Britain, France, the USA and Italy. Each of them, however, brought their own agenda to the negotiating table.

The 'Big Four' delegates at the Paris Peace Conference. Left to right: David Lloyd George (Britain), Vittorio Orlando (Italy), Georges Clemenceau (France), Woodrow Wilson (USA).

The leader of the French delegation was the Prime Minister, Georges Clemenceau. Clemenceau's intention was to weaken Germany as much as possible. France had been invaded by Germany in 1870 and, again, in 1914. Her aim, therefore, was to reduce Germany's military strength and to take control of key territories, such as the Rhineland, to create a buffer state between the two countries. This was in addition to regaining the provinces of Alsace and Lorraine, seized by Germany after the war of 1870. France also wanted Germany to pay for the destruction caused by four years of war on French soil. This would involve not just financial reparations, but also French control of German resources such as the coalfields of the Saar. France was determined to ensure her own safety and had little faith in American talk of a 'fair peace'. 'America', they said, 'is far away, protected by the ocean'.

The leader of Britain's delegation was the Prime Minister, David Lloyd George. Lloyd George was torn in different directions as to how to treat Germany. His party, the Liberals, had split in December 1916 over the conduct of the war and he had led a wartime coalition government. In the General Election of December 1918, held just one month after the war ended, Lloyd George was elected as the leader of a majority Conservative coalition, supported by elements of the Liberals. This was the 'Khaki Election', so called because it was dominated by war-time issues and returning soldiers. The most popular subject matter of the election campaign was to ensure 'Full indemnities and reparation from Germany', to 'Make Germany Pay'. As a politician seeking re-election, Lloyd George was, 'Inclined to shout the popular demand' (Thomas Jones, Assistant Cabinet Secretary).

In private discussions, however, Lloyd George held a more balanced view. There had been no fighting in Britain itself and no devastation of the kind suffered by France. Lloyd George supported the need for reparations as the war had bankrupted Britain. He was, however, conscious of the fact that Germany had been an important trading partner of Britain before 1914 and wanted to help restore her economy so that she could once again trade with Britain. In addition, he was concerned by the spread of Communism in Europe after the Russian Revolution of 1917 and did not want Germany to be so damaged and humiliated that she turned towards Communism. This fear was based in no small part on the Spartacist (a German communist party) rising in Berlin in the winter of 1918-19.

The American delegation was led by the Democrat President, Woodrow Wilson.

The USA had entered the war at a relatively late stage and suffered much less from it than had any of the other Allies. Wilson was also conscious of the diverse ethnic

Spartacist street-fighters in Berlin, November 1918

background of many Americans. In January 1918 Wilson had published a statement that became known as the 14 Points. This called for a diplomatic end to war; for a policy of open agreements between nations; for international disarmament; for self-determination of national boundaries based on ethnic lines. These principles would, he hoped, form the basis for a fair and lasting peace which would help to avoid future wars. Further to this aim, he proposed the formation of a League of Nations so that future conflict could be resolved by discussion and joint action rather than by war.

Not surprisingly, the other members of the Big Four were sceptical of Wilson's idealism. Nor were his views uniformly supported in the USA, where many Republicans and even prominent Democrats opposed his international-ism. In the mid-term elections of November 1918 Wilson lost control of the Senate and the House of Representa-tives, so weakening his political stance in the Paris negoti-ations. Further complications arose when Wilson collapsed with a stroke in October 1919, brought on by a strenuous cross-country campaign to persuade the American people to accept the Treaty of Versailles. His successor as Pres-ident in 1920, the Republican Warren Hastings, rejected the Treaty of Versailles and, with it, the League of Nations because it threatened to involve the USA in future conflicts. The American Senate never achieved the majority needed to ratify the Treaty of Versailles with Germany. The USA was eventually to sign its own peace treaty with Germany in 1921, and, also, with Austria and Hungary.

The final member of the Big Four, Vittorio Orlando, the leader of the Italian delegation, was more peripheral in his importance and impact. Italy had begun World War

1 as the ally of Germany but did not join in the fighting, before changing sides in 1915. This weakened Italy's authority in the negotiations. Prime Minister Orlando was also hampered by his lack of English, by his weak political position in Italy and by clashes over policy with the more dominant, English speaking, foreign minister Sonnino, especially over Italian claims to Dalmatia.

Orlando dramatically left the conference in April 1919, Italian demands having run up against Woodrow Wilson's policy of national self-determination, and was forced to resign days before the signing of the Treaty of Versailles. He was later proud not to have been a signatory! Clemenceau called him 'The Weeper'. Orlando himself said that, 'When I knew they would not give us what we were entitled to … I cried. I wanted to die.'

Clashes of personality, policies and principles shaped the decisions arrived at in a series of 145 hurried and confrontational meetings between the Big Four.

'How did you get on?' Clemenceau was asked after one stormy session with Wilson.

'Splendid,' he replied. 'We disagreed about everything.'

Arrived at by piecemeal decisions, none of the delegates actually read the full *Preliminaries of Peace* until the last minute. Nor was there any discussion of their cumulative effect. Lloyd George later admitted that he had received a complete copy of the treaty only just before it was presented to Germany.

On next page: The main territorial changes made by the Treaty of Versailles (Map by Historicair, adapted by Fluteflute: https://commons.wikimedia.org/w/index.php?curid=5707302)

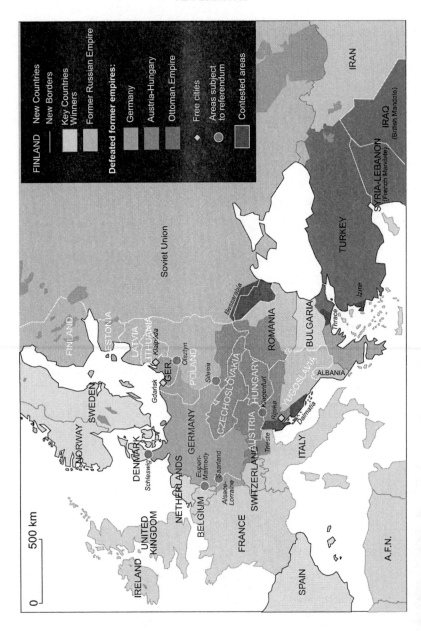

48

Germany was severely punished by the terms of the Treaty of Versailles:

- She was stripped of just over 13% of her territory, including the return of Alsace Lorraine to France, taken after the 1870 war. Most hated by the Germans was the loss of land to Poland. Germany was divided in two by the cession of the 'Polish Corridor' to give Poland access to the sea. The city of Danzig, with half a million Germans, was made into a 'free city' under the League of Nations. Germany cited that this was in breach of Wilson's principles of self-determination of peoples, as was the loss of the Sudeten Germans to Czechoslovakia.

- Although Austria was a wholly German state, it was prohibited from union or Anschluss with Germany. Its seven million population would have made Germany larger than it had been in 1914.

- Germany's military capability was severely reduced so that it would be incapable of offensive action.

German submarine washed ashore at Hastings

Her army was reduced to 100,000 men; her navy reduced in size; her air-force dismantled and prohibited.

- Germany lost all of her colonies. Article 22 of the Treaty of Versailles divided them between the Allied powers. German East Africa, for example, went to Britain.

- Germany had to pay reparations to certain countries who had been damaged by the war. The level of payment was fixed in 1921 at £6.6 billion (equivalent to £284 billion today). This was at a time when Germany's economic output and productivity were weakened by the war and the losses of Versailles. When, in 1922, Germany was unable to pay, French troops invaded the Ruhr region, so triggering the collapse of the German currency.

French soldiers enter the Germany city of Essen as part of their invasion of the Ruhr

- The Rhineland area was to be de-militarised, such that no German soldiers could be placed there. This was intended to act as a buffer between France and Germany. For a limited period it was to be garrisoned by Allied troops.

- Germany lost 75% of its iron ore and 26% of its coal and potash. This included the cession of the Saar coalfields to France for 15 years. A plebiscite would then decide its fate.

At first, Germany refused to sign the terms when they were presented to her on 7 May 1919, not having been allowed to see them before. Germany strongly objected to many of the terms, but especially to Article 231, the War Guilt clause, which they said was an insult to Germany's honour. It stated: the 'Responsibility of Germany and her allies for causing all the loss and damage' during the war. The Allies gave Germany three weeks to accept and threatened to invade Germany unless they signed immediately. Field Marshal Hindenburg was asked whether the army could resist an Allied invasion, to which he replied that it could not. Chancellor Scheidemann stated that the treaty was 'unacceptable' and resigned. His successor, Gustav Bauer, tried to re-negotiate some of the more onerous terms, but the Allies simply repeated their threat to invade. The Treaty of Versailles was, therefore, a 'Diktat', imposed on Germany against her will. This was to give her the moral high ground in the future and ensure the sympathy of British politicians when Germany began to renege on the terms of the treaty.

Historical views are divided as to whether the terms were too harsh on Germany. The economist John Maynard

Keynes, in his book *The Economic Consequences of the Peace* (1919), called it a 'Carthaginian peace', after the intention of Ancient Rome to crush its great enemy, Carthage. He said that the reparations figure was excessive and counter-productive. This is the basis for the popular view that the excessively harsh terms of Versailles ensured the rise of Hitler and the eventual outbreak of World War 2.

Historians' views have since become more balanced.

The terms were less harsh than those that Germany herself imposed on Russia in the Treaty of Brest-Litovsk of 1918 and almost certainly would have imposed on the Allies if Germany had won the war. By 1918 much of the industrial areas of northern France had been destroyed, whereas German industry was still intact. One argument is that the reduction in the size of the German armed forces saved the state so much money compared to the Kaiser's regime that they could have paid reparations more effectively. This is a matter of conjecture given the economic problems faced by Germany in the 1920s, firstly with hyper-inflation in 1923 and then the Wall Street Crash of 1929. Germany did, however, receive substantial financial help from the USA in the form of the Dawes Plan (1924) and the Young Plan (1929) to aid her recovery. When she was allowed to stop paying reparations in 1932 at the Lausanne Conference because of her financial and economic collapse, Germany had actually received more in American loans than she had paid out to the Allies in reparations. After 1933, Hitler spent much more each year on re-arming Germany than the annual reparations figure set in 1921. German opposition to reparations was as much a question of political will as of economic and financial strength.

The main problem was that Germany perceived the Treaty of Versailles to have been excessively unfair and burdensome. This perception of a ruinous and vindictive peace was, ultimately, of more significance than the reality. Above all, they were made to shoulder the blame for World War 1 and not allowed to share in the negotiations. Many Germans criticized the 'Diktat' of Versailles and it was to fuel German nationalism in future years. Much of Hitler's appeal and foreign policy was based on atoning for the humiliation of Versailles. When, in 1936, Hitler re-occupied the Rhineland, his first great gamble, Ramsay MacDonald, former British Prime Minister, said that he was 'pleased' that the Treaty of Versailles was 'vanishing'. This was a view shared by many others. The lack of British response to this clear breach of Versailles was to encourage Hitler to go even further. In 1938 he carried out Anschluss with Austria. When, in 1939, Hitler invaded Poland to regain the Polish Corridor and Danzig, his actions triggered World War 2.

Equally, however, it is too simplistic to claim that the Treaty of Versailles made the collapse of the Weimar Republic and the rise of Hitler inevitable. The Weimar Republic seemed to be gaining strength in the period after 1924. Under its Chancellor, Gustav Stresemann, Germany signed the Locarno Treaties in 1925, guaranteeing not to change her borders with France and Belgium. This was the basis for German acceptance into the League of Nations in 1926. With a new currency, the Rentenmark, the German economy began to recover and the Nazis lost political support. By the eve of 1929, they were reduced to 12 seats in the Reichstag. As much or more blame, it can be argued, lies with the Wall Street Crash and the Great Depression after 1929, something whose roots lay in the rapid expansion of American capitalism in the years after 1918. When the American stock market and economy collapsed in 1929, the USA asked Germany to repay the loans made under the Dawes and Young Plans. It was this that triggered the economic, financial and political collapse in Germany that the Nazis exploited to bring Hitler to power as Chancellor in 1933.

One argument put forward by Andrew Roberts' *History of the English-Speaking Peoples Since 1900* is that the rise of Hitler and the road to World War 2 would have been avoided if the Treaty of Versailles had been much harsher rather than less harsh. For example, by dividing Germany back up into the small states that existed before 1870, when German unification was completed under Bismarck. In reality, this idea would have seemed impractical, even in the charged atmosphere of 1919, and was never seriously considered. Germany was, however, left with a much larger population than France and with potentially greater economic resources. Though divided and weakened, it still had the potential to seek revenge on France once it had recovered.

For many French, the Treaty of Versailles failed to protect France against a resurgent and vengeful Germany. Clemenceau was voted out of office in January 1920 because it was felt that he had failed to protect France's interests. There is some evidence that British officials thought France was greedy at the negotiations. The archives, now available, show that, during the negotiations, France was, in fact, more reasonable than was once argued. Marshal Foch stated that, 'This (treaty) is not peace. It is an armistice for twenty years.'

Whatever the truth of what happened behind the scenes in Paris, the result was an unsatisfactory compromise. Germany was left with a sense of grievance which nationalists such as Hitler were able to exploit. None of the Big Four fully achieved their aims and, for some, the result was political defeat.

Versailles is a settlement about which views will continue to differ. The question is, however, whether any other outcome was likely given the circumstances and the forces at work in 1918 to 1919.

Woodrow Wilson's friend, Edward Marshall House, wrote in his diary in June 1919:

'It is easy to say what should have been done, but more difficult to have found a way of doing it. Perhaps it was inevitable that the outcome of the Paris Peace Conference, the Treaty of Versailles, would be a compromise that satisfied nobody. To those who are saying that the treaty is bad and should never have been made and that it will involve Europe in infinite difficulties ... I feel like admitting it. While I would have preferred a different peace, I doubt very much whether it could have been made.'

CHAPTER 4
The Middle East:
the seeds of future conflict

UNTIL WORLD WAR 1, MUCH OF THE AREA THAT we know as the Middle East was part of the empire of the Ottoman Turks. Already weak and losing control of its empire before 1914, Turkey was known as the 'Sick Man of Europe'. It was partly an attempt to shore up this weakness that had led to Turkey's alliance with Germany at the start of World War 1. The outcome of its involvement in the war

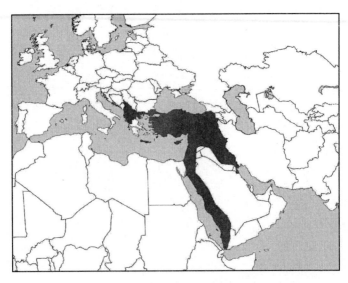

Map of the Ottoman Empire pre WW1

was, however, to prove the opposite of what Turkey had intended. Defeat by the Allies during World War 1, especially by British forces, brought the final collapse of the Ottoman Empire and changed the entire face of the region. It was this collapse and partitioning of the Ottoman Empire between 1918 and 1923 that created the modern Arab world. It was not to prove a stable creation. The settlement made by the victors in the Treaty of Sèvres (1920), as part of the Paris peace treaties after World War 1, fostered an instability that generated much controversy at the time and continues to be a source of conflict today.

The Ottoman Empire was established by the Ottoman Turks from 1299 onwards. At its height it stretched from South East Europe, to the Caucasus and to North Africa. The empire gradually declined in the 19th century. Defeat by the Allies in World War 1, aided by the Arab revolt, led to the final collapse and partitioning of the empire, set out in the Treaty of Sèvres.

It was Britain that played the main role in defeating the Ottoman Turks and bringing about the final collapse of the Ottoman Empire. Britain had strong strategic interests in the Middle East, seeing it as safeguarding the route to India, the 'jewel in the crown' of the British Empire. It was also of growing economic importance because of the discovery of oil in the Middle East in 1908. The reliance on oil for military machines of all kinds, such as oil-powered naval ships, tanks and airplanes, had been highlighted by the demands of World War 1. Alongside the military importance of oil, it was also realized that the internal combustion engine would make oil of vital importance to the civilian economy. Lord Curzon, British Foreign Secretary, denied that oil interests influenced British policy in Iraq, but the archives show differently. Sir Maurice Hanky, Secretary of the British War Cabinet, wrote, as British troops raced towards Baghdad, that, 'Control of these oil supplies becomes a first-class war aim'. Only the discovery of oil in northern Mesopotamia (modern day Iraq) can explain the dash for Mosul by British forces four days after the war with Turkey had ended.

British attempts to defeat Turkey and thereby secure her strategic and economic interests in the region had initially met with limited success. At the start of the war, an Anglo-Indian force had been landed at Basra on the Persian Gulf to protect the vital Anglo-Persian oil pipeline. When this evolved into an attempted advance towards Baghdad, however, it soon ground to a halt. The same fate met the attempt to advance from Egypt into Palestine through the Sinai desert and Gaza. In addition, there was the disastrous Gallipoli campaign in 1915. This was Winston Churchill's plan to land British and Commonwealth forces on the

Gallipoli: a landing pier constructed by the Allies in their attempt to secure a foothold on Gallipoli

Gallipoli peninsular to seize control of the Dardanelles Straits and so open up a direct sea route to Britain's Russian allies.

Military success for the British forces only gained pace from 1917 onwards, when Field Marshal Allenby replaced Sir Archibald Murray as commander of the Egyptian Expeditionary Force and was able to benefit from the allocation

The entry of Field Marshal Allenby into Jerusalem
11 December 1917

of extra resources to the war in the Middle East. This was after a lengthy debate within the War Cabinet as to where the priorities for resources lay between the Western Front and other fronts. Allenby was supported by Lloyd George, who had called for, 'Jerusalem by Christmas'. Allenby also benefited from the effects of the Arab uprising against the Turks which had begun in 1916 and tied down many Turkish troops. British forces entered Jerusalem on 11 December 1917.

By the end of World War 1 British and allied forces occupied Ottoman territory that covered modern day Iraq, Palestine, Jordan, Syria and Lebanon.

It was the occupation of Constantinople by British, French and Italian forces in November 1918 that triggered the final collapse of the Ottoman Empire. Britain had played the main role. France and Italy were lesser players, limited by their relatively minor military involvement. Russia, historically a major influence in the Middle East, was paralyzed by the Bolshevik Revolution of November 1917 and the subsequent civil war. The Turks themselves were too weak to prevent the collapse of their empire.

The partition of the Ottoman Empire was ratified at the Paris Peace Conference when Turkey was made to sign the Treaty of Sèvres in 1920. This was later updated by the Treaty of Lausanne in 1923 after the initial treaty had been rejected by the Turkish nationalists. Between them, these treaties, imposed by the victors of World War 1, oversaw the break-up of the Ottoman Empire, leaving behind only the modern republic of Turkey.

The treaties were, however, shaped by conflicting promises, interests and ambitions.

One of these commitments was the promise made by Britain to the Arabs in order to encourage them in their revolt against Turkish rule. In a series of communications between Sir Henry McMahon, British High Commissioner of Egypt, and Sharif Hussein of Mecca, leader of the Hashemite Arabs, between July 1915 and January 1916, Britain had supported the idea of an Arab uprising, (or awakening, as the Arabs preferred to call it). The Arabs, as they interpreted the negotiations, were promised that, if the Ottoman Turks were defeated, they would be rewarded with British recognition of Arab independence. The Arabs hoped for the creation of a pan-Arab state stretching from northern Syria to southern Yemen. McMahon, however, excluded from the agreement any areas in which France had any interests and stated that it would also only apply to areas which were purely Arab. From the start, therefore, there was room for interpretation and disagreement.

A key role in the leadership and the shaping of tactics of the Arab uprising, which began in 1916, was played by T.E. Lawrence (1888-1935): Lawrence of Arabia.

Thomas Edward Lawrence was the second of four illegitimate children born to the Anglo-Irish landowner T.R. Chapman and Sarah, the governess to Chapman's legitimate children. Lawrence was the alias they adopted when they fled from Ireland to begin a life together. T.E. Lawrence gained his knowledge of Arabic and Arab culture from his travels in Syria studying Crusader castles for his Oxford thesis and then as an assistant on British Museum sponsored archaeological digs in northern Syria before WW1. It was here that he developed his deep sympathy for the Arabs and their culture. On the outbreak of World War 1 in 1914 Lawrence joined the intelligence staff. He had, at first, been rejected for military service as he failed the minimum height requirement of 5'5" (165.1cm), but his background and previous survey work in the Sinai for the military (under cover of an archaeological expedition) made his services indispensable. Lawrence was soon posted to the Arab Bureau at GHQ in Egypt. In June 1916 the Arab revolt against Turkish rule had begun in the Hejaz region of Arabia. Lawrence managed to be included in a meeting with the leader of the revolt, Sharif Hussein of Mecca, and befriended his son, Emir Faisal, who was the commander of the Arab forces. Lawrence became the British Army liaison to Faisal and began to shape Arab tactics and discipline. His greatest successes were in his attacks on the railway line linking Damascus and Medina and in the dramatic seizure of Aqaba. Lawrence convinced the British commander, Allenby, to support the rising with guns, ammunition and gold. With Lawrence's tactics and British support, the Arab rising spread to Trans-Jordan and tied down large numbers of Turkish forces. Lawrence's conscience was torn, however, by his knowledge that the British promise to grant virtually complete Arab independence after the war in return for the rising against the Turks was at odds with the Sykes-Picot Agreement in which Britain and France had agreed to divide up the Ottoman Empire between themselves. He entered Damascus in triumph with Faisal in October 1918, dressed in his Arab robes and even accompanied the Arab delegation to Versailles. Lawrence's efforts to lobby on the Arab behalf earned him a reputation among senior British officials as the enemy within. When British attempts to impose colonial rule on Iraq were met by an Arab uprising in May 1920, Winston Churchill, the new Colonial Secretary, took

Lawrence as an adviser to the Cairo Conference 1921. The outcome was that Faisal, who had been forced out of Damascus by the French, was made King of Iraq and his brother, Abdullah, was made ruler of what became Jordan. This did much to assuage Lawrence's guilt at the British treatment of the Arabs, a guilt that had made him refuse the offer of a knighthood from King George V. Lawrence became internationally famous only after the end of the war. This was the result of the American war correspondent, Lowell Thomas, who had spent time with him in the Middle East. In 1919, Thomas launched a lecture tour in America and Britain about his assignment in the Middle East using photos of Lawrence and a documentary film, 'With Lawrence in Arabia.' The image of the fair haired Lawrence in Arab costume captured the public imagination. Lawrence recounted his adventures himself in his book, *Seven Pillars of Wisdom'*.

He eventually became disillusioned by fame and political intrigue. Seeking to escape notoriety, he enlisted in the RAF as an aircraftman and, for a time, the Tank Corps under assumed names, one of which was T.E. Shaw. This was a nod to his good friend, George Bernard Shaw. Lawrence left the RAF in 1935 but died a few months later when he crashed his motorbike in Dorset while trying to avoid two boys on their bicycles. He was just 46

Lawrence of Arabia in Arab costume (photograph by Lowell Thomas)

years old. Field Marshal Allenby once stated, 'There is no other man I know who could have achieved what Lawrence did.'

At the same time as encouraging and supporting the Arab uprising, Britain and France were also deciding on their own partition of the Ottoman Empire. This was based on the Sykes-Picot Agreement of May 1916, drawn up by Mark Sykes on behalf of the British government and Francois Georges-Picot for the French government. By the Agreement, the Arab provinces of the Ottoman Empire that lay outside the Arabian Peninsula were to be divided into different zones. On a map of the Middle East, the diplomats drew a line in the sand from the Persian border in the north-east to the Mediterranean in the south-west. Sykes described it as running from the E in Acre to the last K in Kirkuk. North of this line were to be zones of French control and influence. The French zones comprised much of modern day Syria and Lebanon. To the south of the line were to be British zones, comprising much of modern day Iraq and Jordan. Like the French zones, one would be under direct British control and one a British sphere of influence and protection. Separate promises were made to Tsarist Russia, who was a minority partner to the agreement.

Northern Mesopotamia, the Kurdish area around Mosul, was initially to lie within a French zone, but the discovery of oil in the area prompted Britain to negotiate its inclusion in the British zone in return for increased oil concessions to France. Mosul was entered and occupied by British troops in November 1918, four days after the end of the war with Turkey. Palestine was, initially, to be under international control, reflecting the importance of its religious sites, but in 1920, as part of the San Remo Conference,

Britain assumed control of the area, which became the British Mandate of Palestine. This was further refined at the Cairo Conference 1921 when Trans-Jordan (modern day Jordan) was separated from Palestine and given its own Arab administration and ruler, under the supervision of a British commissioner.

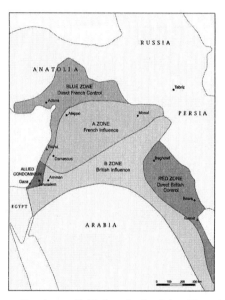

The Ottoman Empire as divided up in the Sykes-Picot Agreement, 1916. Reproduced from www.passia.org with permission (Mahmoud Abu Rumieleh, Webmaster).

There has been much debate as to how far the Sykes-Picot Agreement conflicted with the Hussein-McMahon correspondence. There was, initially, some scope for compromise. In the zones that were placed under direct French and British control, each country was to be allowed to establish such direct administration or control as they desired and thought fit to arrange. In Zones A and B that were designated as French and British spheres of influence, however, the Agreement allowed for the creation of an Arab state or confederation of states under an Arab chief, protected by the colonial powers until such time as they achieved political maturity. Britain did create such regimes in Iraq and Jordan. This possibility was, however, to fall far short of Arab expectations for independence. In any case, further events and agreements were to limit the scope for Arab independence even further.

The terms of the secret agreement were revealed after the Russian Revolution by Lenin, the Bolshevik (Communist) leader. He called it the 'agreement of the colonial thieves'. It was then immediately published in *The Guardian*. The revelations caused Arab dismay and embarrassment for Britain and France.

To add to these conflicting promises and interests came the Balfour Declaration of 1917. In this, Britain promised the Zionist Jews her support to facilitate the creation of a Jewish homeland in Palestine. At that time, Palestine was still part of the Ottoman Empire and settled almost entirely by Arabs.

The Zionist movement was an international Jewish movement set up by the Hungarian Jew, Theodor Herzl, in 1897 against the background of growing anti-Semitism in Europe.

As a major force in the war against the Ottoman Turks, Britain had been pressured by the Zionist movement to support their aim of creating a homeland for the Jews in Palestine.

The promise had been made in a letter by the British Foreign Secretary, Lord Balfour, to Lord Rothschild, leader of the British Jewish community. Britain, the Declaration said, viewed with favor and would facilitate the establishment of a national homeland for the Jewish people in Palestine. The Declaration, used as a yardstick of British policy, had been shaped by the pressures of World War 1. Britain was desperate to gain American support in the war and believed that American Jews played a strong role in influencing government policy.

The settlement made in Paris at the end of World War 1 reflected these conflicting interests and promises.

The Treaty of Sèvres (August 1920), setting out the partition of the Ottoman Empire, was based on the Sykes-Picot Agreement of 1916 and the San Remo Conference of April 1920. The latter had been hurriedly called when Prince Faisal, the leader of the Arab Uprising against the Turks, had led a revolt in Damascus, refusing to acknowledge the claim by the French government to any part of Syrian territory. Prime Minister Clemenceau of France had initially acknowledged the right of the Syrians to govern themselves as an independent nation, but the San Remo Conference, attended by his successor Millerand, confirmed the allocation of League of Nations mandates for the partitioning and administration of the Ottoman territories. The Conference authorized the French mandate to govern Syria and the Lebanon and the British mandate to govern Iraq

Theodor Herzl

and Palestine until such time as these areas were ready for independence. It also re-stated the Balfour Declaration to the Jews.

In effect, the partition of the Ottoman Empire had already been decided before the treaty negotiations began. What the Treaty of Sèvres confirmed were artificial geo-political creations agreed in 1916 and 1920 and put into place at the Paris peace talks. Before then, Greater Syria, as it was sometimes referred to, and Mesopotamia were simply geographical areas within the Ottoman Empire. There were no separate national divisions until they were artificially created by the British and French diplomats when they drew their line on maps of the region. It was already decided, before the Treaty of Sèvres, that France was to be given control and influence of the area to the north of the line, comprising the modern day nations of Syria and Lebanon. Britain was likewise to be given control and influence over the area to the south of the line, which covered Mesopotamia (Iraq), Trans-Jordan (modern day Jordan) and Palestine.

The Treaty of Sèvres also included the responsibility to put into effect the Balfour Declaration which promised the Jews a homeland in Palestine.

The Hashemite Arabs were only rewarded for their role in the Arab Uprising, begun by Sharif Hussein of Mecca, by the international recognition of their kingdom of Hejaz. There was to be no pan-Arab state, which the Arabs believed had been promised to them by Britain in return for rising up against the Turks. In 1921, at the Cairo Conference, called because of Arab resistance in Iraq to British colonial rule, Emir Faisal, the son of Sharif Hussein, who had led the Arab revolt against the Turks, was made King of Iraq and his brother, Abdullah, Emir of Jordan. Both would rule under British control.

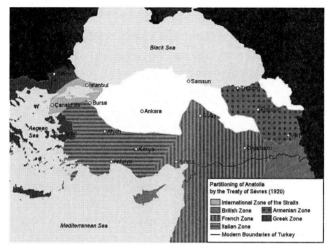

Map of the division of the Ottoman Empire in the Treaty of Sèvres

The dividing up of Greater Syria and Mesopotamia by Britain and France, secretly agreed in the Sykes-Picot Agreement 1916, formalized by the San Remo Conference and carried out by the Treaty of Sèvres 1920, was formally endorsed by the granting of League of Nation mandates (authority to govern on behalf of the League). In reality, these mandates simply recognized the de facto situation that had been created by Britain and France. The French mandate for Syria, for example, came into force in September 1923. By that time, France had already asserted her control over Syria through the use of military force. The mandates committed Britain and France to facilitate the development of independent states in the areas over which they were given control. In practice, both nations were guided by their own interests.

The granting of League of Nations mandates did nothing to ensure stability in the Middle East. The terms of the Treaty of Sèvres lasted barely a year. The effects of the long term instability it created are, however, still with us today.

Acceptance of the Treaty of Sèvres by the Ottoman Sultan, Mehmet VI, triggered the Turkish War of Independence. Nationalist forces led by Mustafa Kemal, who opposed the treaty, overthrew the regime and created a republic. The last sultan, Mehmet VI, left Turkey in November 1922. The Allies were forced to re-negotiate the harsh terms imposed on Turkey. The new terms were agreed in the Treaty of Lausanne 1923. What emerged was the modern day sovereign republic of Turkey, free of the controls imposed by the Allies at Sèvres.

Mustafa Kemal, known as Kemal Ataturk

Even the recognition of the Kingdom of Hejaz in Arabia was to prove short-lived. The British had already reneged on their promises to Sharif Hussein to support the creation of a pan-Arab state under Hashemite rule. In the 1920s they withdrew their support for his regime in favor of the rival al-Saud family, a group who had taken no part in the Arab uprising against the Turks.

The subsequent conquest of Hejaz by the al-Saud forces paved the way for the creation of Saudi Arabia in 1932.

Widespread Arab hostility towards Britain and France arose throughout the region. Those Arabs who had taken part in the uprising against Turkey believed that they had been robbed. They believed that the British had not delivered on their promises of Arab independence: that the British and the other European powers had divided up the Middle East to serve their own imperial interests rather than to serve the interests of the Arab people. They were especially angered by the fate of Palestine, which had been promised to the Jews, despite its Arab population, and occupied by Britain under the League of Nations mandate.

In October 1918, Faisal, the leader of the Arab Uprising against the Turks alongside Lawrence of Arabia, set up an Arab government in Damascus in an attempt to assert Arab rule. Some attempt at negotiations between Faisal and France did take place. Clemenceau even acknowledged the right of the Syrians to unite and to govern themselves as an independent nation. His successor as Prime Minister of France, Millerand, was less responsive. When a Syrian Congress recognized Faisal as King of a 'United Syrian Kingdom' which included the areas of Palestine and Lebanon, this was dismissed by the British and French as 'foolhardy actions' because it threatened their strategic interests and their agreement to control the area themselves. France stated that the Arab recognition of Faisal was null and void and demanded full recognition of the Sykes-Picot Agreement. The San Remo Conference was hurriedly convened. This recognized the mandate of France to govern Syria and Lebanon until they reached political maturity. In July 1920, when Faisal rejected this mandate,

French military forces occupied Damascus and overthrew Faisal and his nationalist government. Millerand declared that Syria would henceforth be held by France, 'The whole of it and forever.' The French mandate was, in reality, to last until 1943 though it was not until 1946, under pressure from Britain, that France finally withdrew from Syria.

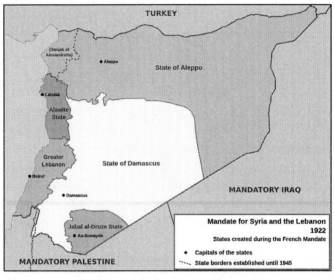

The Syrian and Lebanese mandate, 1922

Once they had ejected the Arab government set up by Emir Faisal, France decided that their control of Syria and Lebanon would best be managed by dividing it up into sub-states. The most contentious of these was the creation of 'Greater Lebanon' in August 1920. This was designed primarily to safeguard the Maronite Christians. In order to create a viable political entity, however, the Christian area around Mount Lebanon was 'allocated' substantial Muslim lands.

72

These additional areas included the coastal cities of Tyre and Sidon and the capital Beirut, with its mixed Christian and Muslim population. The largely Muslim Beqaa Valley was also taken out of Syria and placed within Lebanon. In 1926 this creation by France became the Lebanese Republic. Before this action by France, driven by political and ideological concerns, there had not been any such nation as Lebanon. It was simply an area within the Ottoman Empire. It was not a natural nor stable entity. The Maronite Christians were not even a majority within their own country, comprising as they did approximately 30% of the population. The Muslim areas that had been 'added' to create Greater Lebanon (hence the use of the term 'Greater') strongly opposed their inclusion. The Sunni Muslims, for example, wanted to be part of an independent Syria. The roots of Lebanon's instability down to the present day can be seen in this post-war period of French administration.

British control of Iraq and Palestine also suffered from instability and opposition.

As with Syria and Lebanon, so there had been no Kingdom of Iraq before 1920. Iraq was created by the British from the three vilayets (administrative provinces) of Basra, Baghdad and Mosul. It was a complex and unstable mix of ethnic and religious groups from the start. The Kurds in the north were especially opposed to rule from Baghdad.

An Arab uprising against British colonial rule in Iraq began in May 1920. Its objectives were to gain independence from British rule and the creation of an Arab government. It is estimated that, during the Great Iraqi Revolt, 10,000 people died, including 1,000 British soldiers and administrators. The revolt was eventually quelled by use of the new tactic of aerial bombardment. It was Winston Churchill who authorized aerial bombing of insurgent villages as a means of asserting British control without the need and expense of using large numbers of ground troops. Gertrude Bell, a prominent official of the British administration in Baghdad, wrote that, 'The RAF has done wonders bombing insurgent villages.'

As Colonial Secretary, Winston Churchill was forced by the scale and cost of the Iraqi Revolt to convene the Cairo Conference in 1921. It was felt that Britain needed to control Iraq through more indirect means if it was to avert future rebellions. The Emir Faisal, commander of the Arab uprising 1916-18 that had done so much to defeat Turkey, was made King of Iraq and his brother, Abdullah, Emir of what became Jordan, the region over the river Jordan (hence the name Trans-Jordan) that was separated from the rest of Palestine.

It has been suggested that the making of Faisal as King of Iraq was influenced in part by Britain's guilty conscience. Faisal had been denied the promise of a pan-Arab state made to the Hashemite Arabs in return for taking part in the uprising against Turkey. He had then been ejected from Damascus by French forces. There were, however, other factors involved that, it was hoped, would suit British interests in Iraq. It was hoped that Faisal's role in the Arab uprising and his family's religious authority would make him acceptable to the Moslems of Iraq. It was also noted that, after his experiences in Syria, Faisal, 'Had learned the limits of Arab nationalism and of Europe's superior strength.' He would, Britain hoped, be a more compliant ruler under the British mandate. In a referendum heavily controlled by the British, which also ensured the absence of any viable alternative candidate, Feisal received 96% of the votes to be recognized as King of Iraq.

King Faisal I of Iraq with T. E. Lawrence

Effectively, Faisal was a British puppet ruler. This was confirmed by the treaty imposed on Iraq in 1924. The king would accept British advice on all matters relating to foreign, judicial, military and financial matters. British officials would be appointed to advisory roles in 18 key departments and Iraq would pay half of the costs incurred by Britain in Iraq. The opposition of nationalist and tribal leaders eventually led to the negotiation of a new treaty, which came into effect in 1932. The British mandate ended and Iraq was to enter the League of Nations as a fully sovereign country. Iraq remained, however, a puppet regime. Its Hashemite rulers were only allowed to control events so long as they did not encroach on British strategic and commercial interests. Meanwhile, the seeds of nationalist resistance to colonial rule were growing among the officers within the British-trained army. Iraq was moving towards the actions and events that were to shape its history in the later 20th century and into the 21st.

Another area that was to remain unstable was Kurdistan, the lands historically occupied by the Kurds. These historic lands spread across the frontiers of what became Iraq and the republic of Turkey. The Kurds had hoped that the collapse of the Ottoman Empire would allow the creation of an independent Kurdish state. This was initially negotiated with the Kurds by British diplomats and was even provided for in the Treaty of Sèvres, subject to the agreement of the League of Nations. The inclusion of the Turkish Kurds in any such state was, however, opposed by Kemal Ataturk and the Turkish nationalists. Britain also began to state that the Kingdom of Iraq should include the province of Mosul, that is to say Iraqi Kurdistan, despite strong Kurdish resistance to any unity with Baghdad. A key factor was Britain's desire to exploit the recently discovered oilfields of the region. This was almost certainly why British troops had rushed to gain control of Mosul after the end of the war with Turkey. Angry at what they saw as a string of broken promises, and rejecting British offers of limited autonomy, the Kurds in Iraq rose in rebellion. They were able to briefly declare a Kingdom of Kurdistan between 1922 and 1924, but intensive bombing by the RAF Iraqi Command defeated the rising. Kurdish hopes were finally crushed when the League of Nations gave the mandate over the Kurdish area to British controlled Iraq.

The legacy of regional instability and Kurdish hopes have continued right through to the present day.

Even more contentious was the fate of Palestine after the collapse of the Ottoman Empire. Once again, Britain played a central role in what took place.

The Arabs believed that Britain had promised Palestine to the Arabs as part of an independent Arab nation. This was in return for their support of the Allies by carrying out the Arab uprising against the Turks. The release of classified records has shown that Palestine was not initially excluded from the agreement with Sharif Hussein. A secret memorandum for the British delegation to the Paris peace conference stated that, 'With regard to Palestine, H.M.G. are committed by Sir Henry McMahon's letter to the Sharif on 24 October 1915 to its inclusion in the boundaries of Arab independence'. This was despite the fact that the McMahon correspondence had said that any land, 'That cannot be said to be purely Arab', was to be excluded from any agreement. The Turks had allowed other religious groups to exist in Jerusalem and there had always been some Jews living in Palestine.

The main conflict of interests, however, was that promises to the Arabs were to prove incompatible with promises to the Jews.

In the Balfour Declaration of 1917, Britain had promised to facilitate the creation of a Jewish homeland in Palestine. This was written into the Treaty of Sèvres and into the British mandate to govern Palestine on behalf of the League of Nations. Although the exact commitment made by Britain in the Balfour Declaration was to be subsequently debated and interpreted, what was clear was that Zionist Jews believed that Britain supported increased

Jewish immigration into Palestine. Their numbers grew after 1918 and Jews began to buy up more land to establish their collective farms.

This was bitterly resented by the Palestinian Arabs, many of whom were landless. Britain's role in administering Palestine and ensuring law and order was an almost impossible task. This was apparent when her role was formalized by the granting of a mandate from the League of Nations. The mandate included a commitment on Britain to, 'Secure the establishment of a Jewish home in Palestine.' At the same time, this was to be done without impairing the civil and religious rights of the indigenous Arab people. Riots erupted in Palestine in 1920 and 1921. By the 1930s, with ever more Jews seeking to escape the growth of Fascism in Europe, tensions increased even further. After the Arab revolt of 1936-9, Britain drew up plans for a partition of Palestine between Jews and Arabs. These plans were strongly rejected by the Arabs. The Jews also opposed British attempts to limit Jewish immigration into Palestine. The end of the war and revelations of the Holocaust brought the collapse of the British mandate. In 1948, against a background of spiralling violence, Britain restored control over Palestine to the United Nations (the successor of the League of Nations). When the United Nations announced a partition of Palestine, the Jews declared their state of Israel. The Arabs rejected the partition and went to war with Israel.

So began the complex sequence of wars and terrorism based on Palestine that have shaped the history of this region since World War 2. Their roots, however, lie in the aftermath of World War 1, in the collapse of the Ottoman

Empire and the web of diplomacy and promises spun by Britain.

So where does the balance of responsibility lie for the instability of the Middle East after World War 1, an instability that continued throughout the 20th century and remains into the 21st? There has been much debate as to where the blame lies.

One question now asked is whether the alternative outcomes would have provided greater stability.

If Germany had won World War 1 then the Middle East would have returned to the yoke of harsh and detested Ottoman Turk rule. The problems and instability would simply have been deferred.

As to the fate of the pan-Arab state desired by the Hashemite rulers of Hejaz, only time would have shown. There was no guarantee that Hashemite rule would have been universally accepted, given the complex sectarian, tribal and ethnic divisions within the region.

Alternatively, if the French and British had granted ethnic and religious self-determination as was laid out in the charter of the League of Nations, then the region would have possibly been subjected to the same kind of instability and conflict between sectarian, tribal and ethnic groups that had plagued the Balkans before 1914 and helped to trigger World War 1. It is this instability that has been seen in more recent times in the Middle East as the states created at Paris in the aftermath of World War 1 have begun to break down. It is argued that only the geo-political framework founded by Sykes-Picot and confirmed after WW1 ensured a degree of protection for the religious and ethnic minorities in the region.

There is no doubt, however, that the Sykes-Picot Agreement and the agreements that followed it in the aftermath of WW1 cast a long-lasting shadow over the Middle East. Although the Sykes-Picot Agreement was itself superseded by a long and complex process of treaties, conferences, deals and conflicts at the end of WW1, it became a symbol of the way in which the colonial powers intervened in the Middle East to create political boundaries in their own colonial interests and installed client leaders. It left a legacy of broken promises, a dislike of western interference and a feeling that Arab aspirations had been subsumed by European colonial and economic interests and ambitions. The politicians of Britain and France created political boundaries where none had existed before when they drew their lines onto maps. The contradictions contained within these artificial partitions have been a major cause of the instability that has plagued the Middle East since 1918 and a reference point for Arab nationalism. Their collapse has been one of the stated aims of ISIL (Islamic State of Iraq and the Levant). Its leader vowed to, 'Hit the last nail in the coffin of the Sykes-Picot conspiracy'. In turn, however, the collapse of the geo-political structure that emerged from WW1 has brought an even greater instability to the region.

CHAPTER 5
Russia: the triumph of Communism

BY 1918 THE MOOD WITHIN RUSSIA WAS VERY different from what it had been at the outbreak of World War 1.

In August 1914, as tensions rose throughout Europe and war became imminent, Russia's mounting political and social unrest had been put aside. All sections of society had rallied to Tsar Nicholas II and the defence of Mother Russia against Germany and Austria-Hungary. St Petersburg was even renamed Petrograd because it sounded less Germanic.

In 1917, under the pressure of its involvement in World War 1, Russia underwent two revolutions. The first revolution of February 1917 (March in the Gregorian calendar used in the west) brought the overthrow of the Tsar. The second revolution of October 1917 (November in the west) then saw the seizure of power by the Bolsheviks (Communists), mainly in the key cities of Petrograd and Moscow. In March 1918 Lenin, the Bolshevik leader, made a humiliating surrender to Germany in order to concentrate on securing power throughout Russia. By the Treaty of Brest-Litovsk, Russia lost most of its empire in Eastern Europe. This was followed by a civil war, mass starvation and the imposition of a communist political ideology that was to transform Russia's society and economy as well as those of many other countries around the world.

Tsar Nicholas II

Expectations at the start of World War 1 that the Russian steamroller would crush German forces had quickly been revealed to be ill-founded. Instead, the war had revealed the weaknesses of the Tsarist regime, seen in the military disasters of Tannenberg and the Masurian Lakes. When Nicholas II responded by taking personal control of the Russian war effort in 1915, leaving Petrograd for the Front, the Tsar began to shoulder direct blame for the continued defeats.

The problems caused by the Tsar's absence from Petrograd were compounded by his political incompetence and ideological intransigence. Determined to hold on to his autocratic powers, the Tsar failed to co-operate fully with his duma (state parliament), refusing the call by a 'Progressive Bloc' to form a 'government of public confidence'. Similarly, the regime failed to work fully with the All-Russian Union of Zemstva (regional councils) set up in 1914 to support the war effort.

In the Tsar's absence from Petrograd, the regime was further undermined by lurid stories of the relationship between the rogue holy man Rasputin and the Tsarina, Alexandra. It was a relationship based on her belief in Rasputin's ability to calm and heal the haemophiliac young prince, Alexei, but the secrecy surrounding it and Rasputin's dissolute lifestyle fed wild rumors. Eventually, Rasputin was murdered in December 1916 by Prince Yusupov, who hoped to save the royal family from further scandal, but the damage to its reputation had already been done.

The continuing defeats led to a loss of confidence in the regime and indiscipline among the soldiers. By 1917, with nearly six million either killed or wounded, soldiers were

Gregory Rasputin

beginning to desert or to refuse orders. Added to this was the growing economic hardship in the main cities, especially Petrograd and Moscow. With millions of peasants conscripted, not enough people were left to farm the land. What food there was often failed to reach the cities because the army took priority for food supplies and for the available rail transport. Food shortages and inflation began to cause severe unrest in the main cities. Some women were spending most of the day simply standing in queues for food and other goods. When news of a further reduction in the bread ration became known towards the end of February 1917, anti-government feelings reached a new height.

On Thursday 25 February 1917, International Women's Day, thousands of women took to the streets of Petrograd, calling for 'peace and bread'.

International Women's Day February 1917: women demonstrate in Petrograd to demand increased rations

What had begun that morning as a peaceful demonstration took on a different mood when striking workers from the giant Putilov Iron Works were persuaded to join in the women's protest march. Economic demands soon escalated into political protest against the Tsar and his government. Receiving reports from the Tsarina that played down the unrest, Tsar Nicholas dismissed the riots as a 'hooligan movement' and sent orders for the army to crush the unrest. This was an important catalyst in turning protest into revolution. When some regiments opened fire on the crowds, the mood darkened. The soldiers of the Petrograd garrison had to decide whether to join the people or to fire on them. Many of the troops garrisoned in the city were young reservists, fresh from the villages, who shared the dissatisfaction of the protestors. They were joined in this by their NCOs, who had decided that the time had come to stop firing on the people. One by one, regiments began to join the protest. Officers, fearing for their lives, began to lose control over their troops. As Orlando Figes' *A People's Tragedy* commented, 'The mutiny of the Petrograd garrison turned the disorders … into a full-scale revolution.'

Absent at his military headquarters, the Tsar received a report which stated that, 'The capital is in a state of anarchy. The Government is paralyzed. Transport services and the supply of food have become completely disrupted. General discontent is growing.' When he received this report of the true scale of the unrest, Tsar Nicholas set out to return to his capital but his train was held up by striking workers. Faced with pressure to abdicate from his generals and from the politicians, Tsar Nicholas had no alternative but to agree, both for himself and for his son, Alexei, who was too fragile to rule. When his brother, Grand Duke Michael, refused to take over the reins of power, the Romanov dynasty, which had lasted over 300 years, came to an abrupt end.

85

A parliamentary Provisional Government was set up in Russia. From the start, its hold on power was fragile. Its leaders had emerged from the Tsarist duma, elected before the revolution on a franchise weighted heavily in favor of the upper classes. The soldiers and workers of Petrograd set up a soviet (council) which was soon copied in other major cities and districts throughout the country. Order Number One of the Petrograd Soviet was that no ruling by the Provisional Government was to be accepted if it contradicted the authority of the Soviet. A Dual Authority existed in Russia, one which undermined the authority of the parliamentary government.

The unstable situation in Russia opened the way for the return of the Bolshevik (Communist) leader, Lenin, in April 1917 from exile in Switzerland. Preaching a doctrine of workers' revolution and immediate peace, Lenin was smuggled back into Russia in a sealed train. The train was allowed to pass through Germany because it was in German interests to foment Bolshevik revolution within Russia in order to take her out of World War 1. This would free up troops from the Eastern Front to fight in the west. In 1918 this was exactly what happened, allowing Germany to launch the Spring Offensives on the Western Front.

Lenin's campaign was aided by the weaknesses and mistakes of the Provisional Government. Forced by its reliance on foreign loans to continue involvement in World War 1, the government felt unwilling or unable to introduce reforms or to hold elections while the war continued. It therefore lacked the authority of an elected government and failed to meet the expectation of reform now that the Tsar had fallen, such as for the redistribution of land.

The problems which had beset Russia before the overthrow of the Tsar began to escalate. Food shortages, high prices, deserting soldiers, land seizures and violence in the countryside all increased in scale. Added to this was continued military defeat. The failure of the Summer Offensive by Russia in 1917 led to the threat of a German advance on Petrograd and further undermined the authority of the government. As the enemy advanced, an attempted military coup by General Kornilov was only thwarted at the expense of the government arming the Bolsheviks to defend the city.

Armed and organized, the Bolsheviks offered the only clear alternative to the weak regime of the Provisional Government. Most striking was the decisive leadership of Lenin compared to the weakness of Kerensky, the leader of the Provisional Government.

Lenin offered a deceptively simple but appealing programme of, 'Peace, Bread and Land' and, 'All power to the soviets'. Meanwhile, the Bolsheviks were securing a political base by taking control of the Petrograd Soviet through the efforts of Leon Trotsky and increasing their support in other soviets.

In October 1917 Lenin and the Bolsheviks seized power in Petrograd and Moscow. In the capital it was almost a bloodless coup. Hardly anybody was left that was willing to defend the Provisional Government apart from a small group of cadets and women soldiers who put up little resistance. The heroic Storming of the Winter Palace shown through Eisenstein's film was largely a myth of Bolshevik propaganda. More casualties occurred in the making of the film than in the actual seizing of the palace. In Moscow, the seizure of power was not so easy and a bloody 10 day period of fighting was needed.

One of the great debates surrounding the October Revolution is whether the Bolsheviks seized power in a coup d'état or whether they were swept to power on the back of popular support for their doctrine. Whatever the truth, they benefited from the political vacuum created by the weakness and unpopularity of the Provisional Government.

Alexandr Kerensky, leader of the Provisional Government, 1917

'The Bolshevik': a painting by Boris Kustodiev

Even so, the Bolsheviks' hold over Russia was tenuous, confined to the area around the two main cities and facing political and social opposition even within those areas. The early weeks of the Bolshevik regime were marked by a series of strikes and opposition campaigns in a range of major ministries and government departments. When Trotsky, for example, arrived at the Ministry of Foreign Affairs and declared himself to be their new Minister, he was met by ironic laughter and a walk out by the officials.

Lenin's greatest challenge, therefore, was to impose Bolshevik power throughout Russia.

Lenin immediately began a period of social and economic reform to transform Russia and to win support for the Bolsheviks from the masses. A Land Decree gave the peasants the right to seize land from the gentry without compensation. Workers were given the right to seize factories. Class warfare was encouraged. Anybody accused of being a burzhui (middle class) was liable to be arrested, beaten or robbed. Their homes and businesses were often looted. Though these actions took economic power away from the middle classes, they were actually at odds with Bolshevik ideas which believed that all means of production should be controlled centrally by the state. Industry was eventually nationalized in February 1918 as part of the policy of War Communism, introduced against the background of imminent Civil War. Running factories by workers' committees had proved a disaster.

Lenin and Trotsky (centre) on the second anniversary of the Revolution

Lenin also began to impose a one party state, something that not even all those who supported the October Revolution wanted to see. He, however, had not carried out a revolution in order to share power. Under pressure from many factions, Lenin was forced to hold elections to a Constituent Assembly but was horrified to find that the Bolsheviks won less than a quarter of the seats. He allowed the Constituent Assembly to sit for one day, 5 January 1918, before closing it down by force. He claimed that Bolshevik ideology was a higher form of democracy than that of an elected assembly. 'No revolution', he wrote, 'ever waits for formal majorities'.

In this way, the Bolsheviks crushed the beginnings of parliamentary government in Russia. A national parliament (duma) had been set up after the 1905 Revolution though its power had always been limited by that of the Tsar. The brief period of the Provisional Government after February 1917 was, arguably, the only time that Russia had approached a western-style parliamentary system of government. The Bolshevik Revolution of October 1917, followed by the dissolution of the Constituent Assembly, abruptly ended this experiment in western-style parliamentary government. The German socialist, Rosa Luxemburg, condemned the 'elimination of democracy' in Russia, stating that the 'remedy' was worse than 'the disease it is supposed to cure'. Rosa Luxemburg was herself to be killed in the aftermath of the failed Spartacist (German Communist) rising in Berlin in January 1919.

State autocracy was then extended further by Lenin and the Bolsheviks. The Tsarist system had also used repression, but the Bolsheviks imposed it in a more systematic and efficient manner.

Opposition politicians were arrested and the opposition press closed. The Cheka (Secret State Police) was established as an instrument of terror. The legal system was abolished and replaced by revolutionary justice. State autocracy, one party rule and the denial of civil rights as understood in liberal democracies were to remain key features of communist rule in Russia throughout the time of Lenin, Stalin and beyond.

One of Lenin's first acts was to agree a peace treaty with Germany at Brest-Litovsk so that he could focus on consolidating Communism within Russia. Once the October Revolution had taken place, Lenin had issued The Decree on Peace which reaffirmed his commitment to ending the war. The Russian army began to disintegrate. Soldiers had no desire to die in a lost cause and wanted to return to their villages in order to seize land. Germany exploited this situation by demanding harsh terms. At first, Trotsky, the Russian negotiator, refused to agree to the terms, but Lenin realized that there was no alternative if the Bolsheviks were to secure power throughout Russia. Russia signed the Treaty of Brest-Litovsk on 3 March 1918.

Signing the Treaty of Brest-Litovsk

By the Treaty of Brest-Litovsk, Russia was forced to allow the independence of much of its empire in Eastern Europe built up by the Tsars. Finland, which had been helped by Germany to defeat a Bolshevik rising, remained independent. Estonia, Latvia and Lithuania became independent republics. The Russian-held area of Poland became part of the independent Republic of Poland. The Germans also set up semi-independent governments in Belarus, the Ukraine and Georgia. The territorial losses amounted to one-third of European Russia. Russia had lost approximately 45 million people, one sixth of its population. More importantly, it lost 54% of its industry, including 74% of its iron ore and coal reserves and 27% of its best agricultural land. In addition, it was ordered to pay three billion roubles in war reparations. Patriotic Russians were horrified at what they saw as the loss of large tracts of the homeland. Many joined the opposition against the Bolsheviks because of the national humiliation agreed to by Lenin. The Treaty of Brest-Litovsk was annulled when Germany surrendered at the end of World War 1 and Germany withdrew its occupying forces from the lands that it had gained. This simply left behind a power vacuum. The fate of the region was decided over the next three years in a series of violent struggles, especially the Russo-Polish War that was ended by the Treaty of Riga 1921. Though Bolshevik Russia regained control of the Ukraine and Belarus during the Russian Civil War, Poland and the Baltic states emerged as independent countries. Issues surrounding these lost territories continued to surface throughout the 20th century and remain relevant today.

Contemporary map showing the territories lost by Russia in the Treaty of Brest-Litovsk

The Treaty of Brest-Litovsk had one other effect. The harsh conditions imposed on Russia by Germany were to be used as a justification for the harsh terms imposed on Germany by the Treaty of Versailles.

With peace bought at a terrible price, Lenin was now able to set about gaining control of the rest of Russia. What followed was a bloody Civil War between the Reds (the Communist forces) and the Whites (the anti-Communists) which lasted from 1918 to 1920. Following the economic effects of World War 1, Russia was already on its knees. The Civil War made the situation much worse. It is estimated that the overall death toll, including civilians, was as high as 10 million. Hunger and epidemics contributed to a large percentage of the casualties. Russia was hit by the Spanish Flu pandemic of 1918 to 1919, but the biggest killer was typhus which spread rapidly among the lice-ridden troops and civilian population. It was, above all, a savage and brutal conflict, as were many civil wars later in the 20th century such as in the Balkans and parts of Africa. Some of the brutality is revealed in the novels written about the period, such as Boris Pasternak's *Dr Zhivago*. The Cheka began to increase the scale and intensity of their executions, a policy of class warfare known as 'Red Terror'. They talked of wiping out the middle class entirely. The real purpose was to terrify any who were opposed to the Bolsheviks.

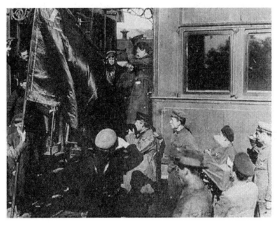

Leon Trotsky on a Red Army train during the Civil War

The eventual Bolshevik victory was greatly aided by Trotsky's organization of the Red Army, based on harsh military discipline. Travelling around Russia in his special train, Trotsky acted as a figurehead for the Reds.

This contrasted with the divisions between the disparate groups fighting on the side of the Whites. Their leaders opposed the Bolsheviks but were often not agreed as to what they were fighting for. There was some Allied intervention in Russia on the side of the White forces but it was limited and half-hearted. Britain sent £100 million of aid to the Whites but nowhere was there much enthusiasm to commit troops. By 1918 the major powers were war weary and there was social and political resistance to involvement. The Labour Party in Britain, for example, believed that Britain should not fight the Russian working class.

One of the most famous events was the execution of the Tsar and his family on 17 July 1918 at Yekaterinburg in the Urals. Lenin claimed that the action had been carried out by local soviets against the wishes of the central government. Documents which have become available to western historians since the collapse of the USSR suggest that it was Lenin who gave the order to execute the Tsar and his family so as to prevent any rescue by the Whites. Lenin deliberately distanced his government from the murders because of the close links between the Tsar and other European royal families. Alexandra, the Tsar's wife, was German. Stories of the possible survival of some of the family, especially Anastasia, surfaced for many years but were not based on fact. The entire family had been shot, their bodies drenched in acid and thrown down a disused mine shaft.

Tsar Nicholas II with the Tsarina Alexandra and their children, Olga, Tatiana, Maria, Anastasia and Alexei, in 1913

Economic recovery from the effects of Revolution and Civil War was to prove very slow, necessitating twists and turns in the policies of the Bolshevik government.

The winter of 1920 – 21 saw widespread popular unrest in response to the effects of food shortages and 'militarized' factories that resulted from Lenin's War Communism. There was a wave of strikes and even a mutiny by the Kronstadt sailors. In March 1921, faced with economic collapse and widespread rebellion, Lenin was forced to relax War Communism and allow some private enterprise in his New Economic Policy (NEP). Peasants were allowed to sell surplus grain, small businesses reopened and the ban on private trade was removed.

This relaxation, however, did not distract from the fact that Russia's economy had been transformed by the effects of World War 1 and the two revolutions that followed. Even in the NEP, the state retained control of large-scale industries, transport and banking. Then, in 1928, came the 'Great Turn' by which centralized control was extended across the entire economy.

In January 1924 Lenin died after a period of illness and was replaced by the even more autocratic Stalin as the next 'Red Tsar'.

Yossif Dzugashvili, known as Stalin (centre), with fellow Bolsheviks (left to right) Antipov, Kirov and Shvernik, who one by one were removed from official versions of this picture.

Stalin was determined to cast the NEP aside. Industry had not developed much beyond its pre-1914 level and agriculture was still backward. Above all, Stalin wanted to build up Russia's military strength and self-sufficiency in manufactured goods through rapid industrialization. To do this, he needed to take agricultural production out of the hands of the peasants. Only in this way could the state set targets for agricultural production and sell surplus grain in order to finance industrial investment. In 1928, confident of his hold on power, Stalin instigated his 'Five Year Plans' for industry and agriculture based on strict central control of the economy. Private enterprise was banned. Agriculture was then collectivized and the private farmers (kulaks) persecuted. In this way, Bolshevik ideology was finally applied across the entire economy. Russia's economy was to remain centrally controlled for much of the 20th century, until the collapse of Communism once again freed up its assets for private ownership.

Russia's political system had been transformed by revolution and civil war in the aftermath of World War 1. Firstly the Tsarist regime had been overthrown in the 1917 February Revolution and then the parliamentary Provisional Government in the October Revolution. The Bolshevik victory in the civil war had imposed communist rule throughout Russia. By 1924 Russia was governed by a centralized, one-party dictatorship that did not permit anybody to challenge its power. All major decisions were taken by a powerful communist elite set up in 1919, the Politburo, which consisted of seven to nine members, headed by a strong leader. This system was to remain for much of the 20th century.

Though Russia saw a change of ideology, institutions and ruling personnel, western historians also point to the similarities between the Bolshevik regime and that of the Tsars. In many ways the rule of the Bolsheviks was a continuation of the absolutist tradition of the Tsars. Marxism (the ideas of Karl Marx on which the Bolshevik ideals of Communism were based) was just as intolerant of opposition as Tsardom had been. The dissolution of the Constituent Assembly in 1918, the Terror, the civil war and the crushing of the Kronstadt revolt were all evidence of the absolutism and intolerance of Bolshevik rule. Just as the Tsar's absolute power had been justified by his right to rule from God, so the absolutism of the Bolsheviks was justified by their political ideology. It was the mission of the Bolshevik party to lead and guide the Russian people towards their historical destiny of a proletarian (workers') state. This, said Lenin, justified the 'dictatorial powers of one man'. Lenin used the term 'democratic centralism' to describe the enforcement of power from the centre. In reality, democracy as interpreted by Lenin did not require a majority of support but, instead, was based on the historical right of the Bolsheviks to rule Russia and to guide its people. The rule of the Tsars had been replaced by that of 'Red Tsars'.

Communism as an ideology had a great impact on the wider world throughout 20th century.

Trotsky had argued that Russia should promote 'permanent revolution', that is to say workers' revolutions in other countries. Stalin rejected this argument in 1928, believing that the priority was to consolidate 'Socialism in one country'. His decision closely mirrored the move from Lenin's NEP to the Five Year Plans. The priority, he said, was to consolidate and develop the revolution within Russia.

Even so, communist parties and ideas did play a major role in the history of other countries. Nowhere was this more evident than in Germany where the communist Spartacist Party had attempted to seize power in the winter of 1918 to 1919. Though this was defeated, the German Communists remained a powerful force. It was their growth in the Reichstag after the economic collapse of 1929, triggered by the Wall Street Crash in the USA, that prompted many Germans to vote Nazi and led to a group of powerful figures making Hitler Chancellor (P.M.) in January 1933. They believed that only Hitler could save Germany from the threat of Communism.

The period after 1939 then saw a reassertion and extension of communist control over much of Eastern Europe.

After signing the Molotov-Ribbentrop Pact with Nazi Germany on the eve of WW2, Russia invaded Poland in September 1939. In 1940 it annexed the Baltic States, Eastern Poland and Bessarabia, thus overturning most of the territorial losses incurred at Brest-Litovsk. Only Finland successfully resisted Russian invasion, firstly in the Winter War of 1939 to 1940 and then in the Continuation War of 1941 to 1944. In this war Finland was supported by Nazi Germany after the German invasion of Soviet Russia in Operation Barbarossa 1941. Finland was, therefore, characterized as one of the Axis Powers alongside Germany, Italy and Japan, though they termed themselves co-belligerents rather than military allies, fighting against the same enemy as Nazi Germany.

As its armies defeated and pushed back Nazi forces in the late stages of the Second World War, Russia further extended its political control in Eastern and Central Europe, including countries such as Hungary, Czechoslovakia and Eastern Germany. An 'Iron Curtain', a description used by Winston Churchill, was imposed, dividing Eastern and Western Europe. Moscow set up political regimes in all of the countries it controlled to ensure that they would follow a narrow Communist, pro-Russian line. Some countries were easier to control than others. The most difficult was Poland. Stalin once said that, 'Imposing Communism on Poland was like putting a saddle on a cow'. Any attempt by these countries to free themselves from Russia was crushed by military intervention. This was seen in Hungary in 1956 and in the Prague Spring of 1968 in Czechoslovakia.

Then, in the 1980s, Mikhail Gorbachev, the new leader of the USSR, began reforms of 'glasnost' (political openness) and 'perestroika' (economic restructuring) in an attempt to strengthen Russia. Centralized control and one-party rule, it was increasingly felt, were causing Russia to fall ever further behind the West. The instability that followed was to bring both the collapse of Russia's control of Eastern and Central Europe from 1989 onwards, beginning with the collapse of the Berlin Wall, and the eventual collapse of Communism within Russia itself.

Mikhail Gorbachev with President Reagan and Vice-President Bush

The effects of the Russian Revolution also spread beyond Europe. Other countries around the world, such as Cuba and China, adopted variants of Communism throughout the 20th century. The period after WW2 was the era of the Cold War between the ideologies of Communism and Liberal Democracy. At times this threatened war, such as the Cuban Missile Crisis (1962) and, at other times, brought actual war, as in Korea (1950-53) and Vietnam (1955-75). Today, there are said to be five remaining Communist regimes. These are China, Vietnam, Laos, Cuba and North Korea. The latter remains, perhaps, the clearest example of an autocratic political system and centralized economy. Others, such as Vietnam, Cuba and China have all adopted elements of market capitalism to meet the economic challenges of the modern world.

The impact of the World War 1 on Russia and the political and social changes that took place in the aftermath of war were, without doubt, one of the great influences on 20th century history. Their effects are still with us today, within Russia, throughout Europe and in the wider world.

103

CHAPTER 6
The United States of America:
the USA turns in on itself

IN THE AFTERMATH OF WORLD WAR 1 THE AMER-
ican people rejected the international idealism of their
Democratic president, Woodrow Wilson, and elected the
Republicans into power with an overwhelming majority.
Republican policies reflected the hostility of the majority
of Americans to any involvement in another major conflict
such as World War 1. American foreign policy after 1918
was based on an avoidance of entanglements that might
involve the USA in another war. The Republicans also
believed in a policy of laissez-faire (leave alone), in which
big business was allowed to manage the economy with
little interference from the federal government. The effects
of this political and economic move to the right were to be
highly significant both for the USA and for the world in the
period leading up to World War 2.

Responding to Germany's resumption of unrestricted
U-Boat warfare and interference in Mexico, President
Wilson had taken the USA into World War 1 in April
1917. After committing substantial troops to the final
stages of the war and helping to tip the balance in the
Allies' favor, the USA emerged as one of the victors of the
conflict. Wilson then played an important role in helping
to shape the Paris Peace Conference as one of the Big Four,

alongside Clemenceau of France, Lloyd George of Britain and Orlando of Italy.

Calling for a just and fair peace, which he described as 'peace without victory', President Wilson drew up 14 points to act as a guideline for the Paris peace negotiations. Their aim was to remove the factors which, he felt, had led to the outbreak of World War 1. Submitted to the Senate in January 1918, they called for, amongst other things, an end to secret agreements between nations and an end to arms races and rivalry at sea. They also called for the self-determination of peoples and for the setting up of an association of nations to protect peace in the future. This was to be the basis on which the League of Nations was created, the forerunner of the modern United Nations.

These ideals clashed with the diplomatic priorities of the other Allies. Georges Clemenceau, the French premier, was determined both to punish Germany for the damage done to France and to ensure that Germany would be made too weak ever again to attack France. Wilson was forced to compromise on many of his ideals, though he did manage to moderate some of the French demands. The Rhineland, for example, was demilitarized (not allowed any German troops) rather than completely detached from Germany as France had originally intended.

President Woodrow Wilson

Wilson returned to the USA a frustrated and disappointed man, only to find that the mood in his own country had swung against international involvement and commitments. The journalist William Allen White wrote that the American people were, 'Tired of issues, sick at heart of ideals and weary of being noble'.

With a majority of senators (the 'irreconcilables') blocking ratification of the Treaty of Versailles, Wilson decided to go over their heads and appeal directly to the American people through a cross-country speaking tour. Wilson's physician warned him of the dangers to his health that such a strenuous tour would present. The pressures of taking the USA into World War 1 and of negotiating peace had left Wilson a sick and weak man. Wilson rejected the warning, stating that, 'I cannot put my personal safety, my health, in the balance against my duty.' The tour had to be cancelled when Wilson suffered a 'complete breakdown'. In October 1919, soon after his return to Washington, he then suffered a major stroke which left him paralyzed down his left side and impaired his vision. For months, the president remained in his bedroom, barely able to sign his own name. All contact was through his wife, Edith, who would take papers in to him and return with verbal instructions or a scrawled signature on a piece of paper. Edith called it her 'stewardship'. She has since been described as the first woman president for her role during this period.

With the president enfeebled and hidden from the public, the Democrats chose James M. Cox as their candidate in the 1920 election campaign. Even he prevaricated over the League of Nations because it could commit the USA to take part in any war declared by the League. His Republican opponent, Warren Harding, virtually ignored

Cox and campaigned against the ideals that Wilson stood for.

Warren Harding, 29th President of the USA, with his wife. (On August 23 1923 he died suddenly in the middle of a conversation with her.)

Harding won an overwhelming victory, the largest popular vote margin since the unopposed election of Monroe in 1820. It was a victory that was based on a repudiation of Wilson's internationalism and idealism. Harding's campaign promise was a return to 'normalcy' – normal life as it had been before the war. The American public had rejected Wilson's view of the role of the USA in the world. Most bitter in their opposition were the American Roman Catholic Irish and Americans of German background. The former were opposed to any support of Britain after the crushing of the Easter Rising in 1916 and the ongoing War of Independence in Ireland. The latter felt that Wilson had failed to protect and support Germany at Versailles.

In March 1920 the Republican majority in the Senate rejected both the Treaty of Versailles and the League of Nations because they saw it as a commitment to future American involvement in world conflict.

The USA played no part in the League of Nations. American absence from the League was to prove one of the crucial factors that weakened it from the start. Without American support, it proved difficult for the democratic nations such as Britain and France to resist the growth of militarism and autocracy in Japan, Italy and Germany between the wars.

American foreign policy after World War 1 is often described as one of 'Isolation'. This is not entirely accurate. As a major economic, political and even military power, some co-operation between the USA and other nations was both inevitable and necessary. The basis of American policy after 1918 was, however, co-operation without commitment. The Dawes and Young Plans provided American loans to Germany to help its economic recovery, so enabling trade between the two countries. The USA took the lead in negotiations on naval disarmament in the 1920s. In 1928 it signed the Kellogg-Briand Pact with over 60 countries in which it was agreed that war was not the best way to solve problems. Even this agreement, however, did not commit the USA to action of any kind and was, therefore, supported by most leading isolationists.

Nowhere were the limits of American commitment clearer than in its response to the growing military aggression of fascist dictators in the 1930s. By this time, isolationist tendencies had been reinforced by the Depression, which deflated American confidence in its ability and willingness to influence events elsewhere. The Depression also increased distrust in the role of bankers, businessmen and financiers. The Nye Committee concluded that these 'merchants of death' had led the USA into war in 1917 for their own interests. President Hoover re-stated American policy when he said that, 'We should co-operate with the rest of the world so long as that co-operation remains in the field of moral pressure ... that is the limit'.

His successor, President F.D. Roosevelt, did make attempts to gain the power to place pressure on aggressors in international conflicts in consultation with other nations. He likened international aggression to a disease which must be quarantined. His efforts, however, ran into strong opposition from the leading isolationists in Congress. Though the USA expressed its disapproval of aggressive actions such as the Japanese invasion of Manchuria and the Italian invasion of Abyssinia in the 1930s, it made no commitment to involvement or intervention. Instead, the American Congress passed a series of Neutrality Acts between 1935 and 1937 which banned the export or loan of arms and armaments to countries at war. This served only to help the Fascist dictators. American isolation from direct involvement in international conflict was only ended by the Japanese attack on the American naval base of Pearl Harbor in December 1941. The USA entered World War 2 on the Allied side and has continued to play a proactive role in world affairs since then. This has been in marked contrast to the influence of World War 1 on American foreign policy.

American society in the years after 1918 was driven mainly by internal factors. It could not however, isolate itself completely from the external world.

In 1919, the USA was gripped by a 'Red Scare'. This was a nationwide fear that Communists and anarchists were plotting to overthrow the American way of life. The reasons were both external and internal. In November 1917 Russia had undergone a Communist Revolution and there were fears that its radical ideas might spread to the USA. In 1919 the Communist Party of America was formed by a small group of radicals. The main reason for believing in the Red Scare, however, was the way that the media and the authorities viewed a wave of strikes that gripped the USA at the end of the war. The reason for the strikes was because of the downturn in the economy immediately after peace was declared. With approximately nine million people working in war industries and four million in the armed forces, there was certain to be some dislocation. Wages and working conditions came under pressure. In 1919 alone four million workers went on strike, including 100,000 members of the Boston Police Force. One of the main unions organizing the strikes was the International Workers of the World (IWW) or 'Wobblies' as they were known because of their opposition to involvement in the war. The media and the authorities labelled the strikers as 'Reds' and denounced the strikes as 'plots to establish Communism'.

Boston Police with a haul of 'subversive' literature confiscated during the 'Red Scare' of November 1919

In this charged climate there was a series of bomb scares. In April 1919 the Post Office intercepted 36 bombs addressed to prominent members of the American establishment. In June, bombs simultaneously exploded in eight cities across the United States, including one at the home of the Attorney General, Mitchell Palmer. In 1920, a bomb exploded on Wall Street and another at the J.P. Morgan bank.

The authorities responded vigorously. Using powers provided by the 1918 Sedition Act to deport politically undesirable people, a series of raids took place, known as the Palmer Raids. On 2 January 1920 alone more than 4,000 suspected radicals were arrested across 33 cities. A General Intelligence

Mitchell Palmer

111

(anti-radical) Division of the Bureau of Investigation was set up with J. Edgar Hoover as its head. Hoover was to go on to become Director of the FBI. In December 1919, 249 arrested radicals who were found not to be American citizens (and so able to be deported) were placed on an old troopship, christened the *Soviet Ark*, which sailed from New York to Finland. Hoover and Palmer promised the American people that there would be more such ships.

J. Edgar Hoover, Director of the FBI 1924-72, in the early 1930s.

In May 1919 the American Legion was formed, an association of ex-servicemen, to protect the American Constitution and way of life. By the end of the year it had one million members. Though mostly confined to peaceful activities, in the charged atmosphere of 1919 some of its members took the law into their own hands. A common saying of the time was, 'Leave the Reds to the Legion'.

One of the most controversial events was the arrest and trial of two immigrant Italian radicals, Nicola Sacco and Bartolommeo Vanzetti, in May 1920. The men were arrested on suspicion of taking part in an armed robbery in which two people had died. Both were armed when arrested and in their car were radical pamphlets. Although no evidence was presented to link them directly to the crime and 107 witnesses stated that they had seen the men elsewhere at the time of the robbery, Sacco and Vanzetti were found guilty. Another man, Celestine Medeiros, later admitted to the crime, but the radical Italian immigrants were executed in August 1927.

Then, as suddenly as it flared up, the Red Scare died away. The mood began to change when twelve prominent lawyers declared the Palmer Raids to be 'illegal acts'. Fear turned to ridicule when Palmer predicted that a Communist revolution would begin on 1 May 1920 and nothing happened. The press had initially supported the arrests and deportations. *The Washington Post*, for example, had written, 'There is no time to waste on hair-splitting over the infringement of liberty.' By 1920, the same press began to question the excesses and legality of the raids. There were to be no more Soviet Arks, though over 500 more of those rounded up were deported by regular means. The spate of bombings across America ended as suddenly as they had begun. Surprisingly, nobody was ever indicted for them. The Red Scare simply faded away.

The Red Scare of 1919 set a pattern which was to be repeated throughout the 20th and into the 21st centuries. The main fear for much of this period remained that of the Communist threat. The most famous was the second 'Red

Senator Joseph McCarthy

Scare' 1947-57, often called McCarthyism after the Senator who, in 1950, famously produced a list of Communists working within the establishment.

Prompted by Russian occupation of Eastern Europe after WW2, the fear of a nuclear arms race and the creation of the Communist People's Republic of China, McCarthy's accusations and the hearings before the House Un-American Activities Committee (HUAC) were a central feature of American life after WW2. Actors and writers were particularly prominent in being summoned before the Committee, beginning with the 'Hollywood Ten' in October 1947. Refusing to answer the question, 'Are you now, or have you ever been a member of the Communist Party?' because they saw it as a denial of their rights under the constitution, the Ten were sentenced to one year in jail for contempt and barred from working in the motion picture industry. Walt Disney and Ronald Reagan, at that time president of the Screen Actors' Guild, were prominent in promoting anti-Communism in the industry. Other artists were later placed on the Hollywood blacklist, which lasted until 1960.

In 1919 and, again, in the McCarthy era the level of fear matched that of Al-Qaeda in the aftermath of 9/11. Today we continue to live in a world that is dominated by perceived radical threats based on political and religious ideologies. The summer of 1919 in the USA set a pattern which has continued to the present day.

While the USA was gripped by its fear of Communism in 1919, it was also going through a summer of racial violence and unrest. This too was to set a pattern for the century of racial struggle and violence that was to follow.

The roots of the struggle and the unrest lay in the effects of World War 1 and its ending on the lives of African Americans.

The war was an important catalyst to a large-scale movement of African Americans from the South to the industrial cities of the North, such as Chicago, New York and Detroit. In what became known as the 'Great Migration' some 500,000 African Americans left the poverty and inequalities of life in the South. Many worked on cotton plantations, whose economy had been weakened by a boll weevil infestation, by increased competition from other countries and, also, from new synthetic fibres. In the South they were subject to strict segregation and treated as second class citizens through the imposition of a series of laws known as 'Jim Crow'. Racially inspired lynchings were a common feature of life in the American South.

War had boosted industrial demand, creating the need for additional workers in the factories and stockyards of the northern cities. With cheap foreign labour from Europe no longer available, employers looked to southern workers. The prospect of higher wages and improved living conditions drew many African Americans to move to the North. By 1918 the racial balance of many northern cities had been changed forever, with significant results for the future.

At the same time, many thousands of African Americans had responded to the entry of the USA into World War 1. Some resisted enlistment, seeing President Wilson's call that, 'The world must be made safe for democracy,' as hypocritical when they lacked political equality themselves. One resident of Harlem quipped that, 'The Germans ain't done nothing to me'. The National Association for the Advancement of Colored People (NAACP) held a silent protest in

New York with the demand, 'Mr President, why not democracy for America?' Most African Americans, however, chose to show their patriotism to support their claim for legal equality. Some 370,000 joined the army.

They were not treated equally. Most were allocated to service units in mixed regiments, spending the war digging ditches, cleaning latrines and working on the docks. There were two African American combat divisions. One was placed under French command and served with distinction. Many of its soldiers were decorated by the French. The other remained under American command. Its soldiers and performance in battle were subjected to racial prejudice. One report stated that African American soldiers were 'unfit for command in combat'. Most victimized were the small number of African American officers, many of whom

A group of African American soldiers returning from service under French command in WW1. All were awarded the Croix de Guerre for bravery

were subject to bogus charges so that they could be removed from post.

Despite these limitations, their experience in WW1 transformed the lives of many African Americans. They met North and West African soldiers. They were treated with respect by French civilians. Over 200,000 crossed the Atlantic and experienced new places. One soldier commented, 'It changed my outlook on life.' Many were radicalized by the war, determined to combat white racism and to translate war service into social and political change. The African American community took pride in their achievements. A crowd of 250,000 onlookers watched the 396th Infantry Regiment, the 'Harlem Hell fighters', on their homecoming parade.

Instead of bringing change, however, WW1 and the period after 1918 brought increased racial tension and riots.

The Great Migration was itself a cause of tension as the balance of urban populations began to change. Chicago's black population, for example, doubled during World War 1, from 50,000 to over 100,000. The migrants often experienced residential segregation, substandard living conditions and job discrimination. *The Chicago Property Owners' Journal* of 1920 stated that, 'Niggers are undesirable neighbors and entirely irresponsible and vicious.' The economic slump in the immediate post-war period triggered not just a Red Scare but also a surge of violence against African Americans. In many places the African Americans were competing for jobs with other poor communities such as the Irish Americans and tensions rose. In the South, lynchings increased from 64 in 1918 to 83 in 1919. The Ku Klux Klan, which had revived in 1915, spread rapidly in this period. By 1924 it had 4.5 million members before it began a decline in 1925 when its Grand Wizard was convicted of a sexually motivated murder.

The result was a series of race riots across the country in cities such as Washington D.C. and Chicago. In all, there were riots in 22 towns and cities across the USA in the summer of 1919. The riots in Chicago began when an African American bather drifted onto a white area of the beach and drowned after being hit by stones. Violence broke out in the 'Black Belt' of Chicago, mainly initiated by gangs of Irish Americans. In all, some 38 people died in Chicago that summer (23 African Americans and 15 whites). Many hundreds of African Americans were left homeless after their homes were looted and burnt.

In the aftermath of the Chicago race riots, summer 1919.

Across the USA some 120 people were killed in the riots. African Americans called it the Red Summer, a link to the Red Scare then taking place, referring not to the fear of communism but to the blood that was being shed. In several cities federal troops had to be called in to restore order. African Americans also became more politicized and war veterans more prepared to defend themselves against white violence. By 1919 the NAACP had 300 branches and 90,000 members. The scene had been set for the 20th century campaign by African Americans for racial equality.

Economic and financial developments in the USA after the end of WW1 were to have great significance for Europe and the wider world.

In the period after 1918 the American economy began the rapid capitalist and stock market expansion, known as the period of the 'Roaring 20s', which ended in the Wall Street Crash of 1929. This event was to play a crucial role in the coming to power of Hitler and the origins of WW2.

Although there was a short term economic slump immediately after the war ended in 1918, American economic growth had been stimulated and strengthened by the war. Its industries were able to benefit from the disruption caused to its economic rivals by involvement in the war and the USA began to dominate markets that had been controlled by others before 1914. One example was the growth of the American chemical industry to replace Germany in world markets. The impact of World War 1 in helping to establish American economic supremacy was, arguably, one of the war's main effects.

Economic growth was helped by the pro-business policies of the Republican governments after 1920. William Harding's aim was to facilitate a return to 'normalcy'. His successor, Calvin Coolidge, stated that the, 'Chief business of the American people is business'. Republican policies were designed to promote and protect American business-men and then leave them to get on with creating wealth.

The Tariff Act of 1922 made imported foods more expensive and protected American business against foreign competition. Harding began a policy of tax cuts in the belief that the American people would spend their extra money on American goods and the wealthy would be better able to invest in business. The top rate tax was cut to 25%. The underlying philosophy of the Republican governments was that of laissez-faire – leaving the bankers and businessmen to run their own affairs. The Transport Act of 1920, for example, returned the control of the railways to private management.

Nowhere was the philosophy made clearer than in the tolerance of trusts. These were super-corporations which dominated sectors of industry. Wilson and the Democrats had fought against the trusts, believing it was wrong for one company to have almost complete control over a sector of the economy. The Republicans believed that the 'captains of industry' such as Carnegie (steel) and Rocke-feller (oil) knew better than the politicians how to increase the nation's wealth.

The result was a rapid expansion of the American economy, driven by a boom in consumer goods. Middle class Americans began to change in their underlying philosophy. Before 1914, it was thought that thrift was to be commended. By the post-war period a new gener-ation began to believe that the right thing to do was to spend their money on houses and consumer goods of all kinds. Industry responded to the growing demand by producing consumer goods on an unprecedented scale. At the forefront was the automobile industry, making use of the mass-production methods pioneered by Henry Ford to produce the Model T Ford at an affordable price for many.

Part of the assembly line for the Model T Ford, 1913

Consumers were helped in their convictions by the development of a powerful advertising industry and by the availability of hire purchase. Even if they couldn't afford to buy the goods, a small deposit secured them the credit to buy immediately. Banking was allowed to expand with no supervision to meet the growing demand for credit. The banks happily loaned unrealistic amounts of money in the belief that economic growth was here to stay.

From the start, however, the boom was imbalanced.

The farming industry did not share in the prosperity of the industrial cities. New farming methods and technology had greatly increased production but American farmers lacked access to the world markets that would buy this surplus. In reaction to American tariffs, other countries had put up their own barriers to American trade. At the same time, the USA faced growing competition from cheap Canadian wheat. Farm income fell from $22 billion in 1919 to $13 billion by 1928 as many farm prices fell by 50%. Rural banks collapsed as bankruptcies increased. Many unskilled workers, especially African American workers, began to leave the land to search for jobs in the cities. By 1920, for the first time, more Americans were living in cities and towns than in the countryside.

US agricultural scene from the 1920s

Many traditional industries also suffered from the imbalanced pace of change. Coal, for example, faced growing competition from oil and electricity. The USA experienced a coal strike in 1922. Many of the coal workers and their families formed part of the poor white underclass.

The prohibition of alcohol, which was enforced through-out the USA in 1920 by the Volstead Act, seemed to typify the inconsistencies of this period. The temperance movement (against the consumption or sale of alcohol) had a long history in the USA. In 1851, for example, Maine had passed an act to ban alcohol, which was soon joined by twelve other states. The Anti-Saloon League was able to exploit World War 1 by connecting beer and brewers with Germans. Against a background of increased propaganda, the government was helpless to prevent the passing of the Eighteenth Amendment to the constitution which prohib-ited the production, sale or transport of alcohol in the USA. The Volstead Act was then passed to enforce the amend-ment. The ban on alcohol served, however, only to fuel an illegal industry that made immense wealth for criminals

Disposal of alcohol during Prohibition

such as Al Capone. In breaking the law by setting up illegal drinking dens or 'speakeasies' he was meeting the needs of the American people. By 1925 there were said to be more speakeasies in America than there had been saloons in 1919.

Al Capone in 1930

Capone alone made $60 million a year from his speak-easies. Despite his association with gangland murders and corruption, Capone was actually a popular figure in Chicago, such was the American public's ambivalent attitude towards the law.

The boom of the Roaring 20s, which began after World War 1, was destined to collapse. It was based on the consumer demand of the middle classes, something which was certain to be finite in its scope. There was a climate of recklessness and risk, reflected in the obsession with speakeasies and jazz. It was driven by the belief of the younger generation that they had a right to prosperity and did not need to wait to acquire the trappings of material wealth. Meanwhile, there was an under-class of poor whites and African Americans who failed to gain access to the new prosperity. The willingness to take risks and the belief that wealth would continue to increase was reflected in the growth of speculation in buying shares on Wall Street, the

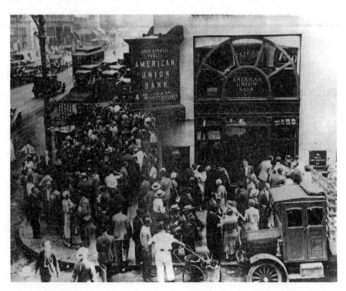

Run on American Union Bank, Black Tuesday 1929

American stock market. Many saw share dealing as an easy way to getting rich. In 1920 there were four million share owners in America. By 1929 there were 20 million.

Then, by 1929, some of the consumer led industries began to falter. Suddenly confidence began to ebb. As stock market prices began to fall, people tried to sell their shares and what began as a trickle became a flood. Banks, which had lent vast amounts on credit during the boom, began to fail. People stopped consuming as they lost confidence and the slump became self-fulfilling. Industries laid off workers. Unemployment rose and wages fell. By 1933 there were 14 million unemployed in the USA and 5,000 banks had gone bankrupt.

Not just the USA suffered. The Depression spread to Europe and beyond. Japan, for example, was badly affected. The financial and economic collapse that took place there was, perhaps, one cause of Japan's growing militarism and expansionist policies of the 1930s. Nowhere was worse hit than Germany when her banks were asked to repay the loans they had been given by the USA in the 1920s. The collapse that followed brought not only the downfall of the German economy after her own economic revival in the later 1920s but also a political collapse. The Democratic Weimar Government could not cope with the instability that followed the stock market and banking collapse. Faced with the growth of the Communist threat among unemployed workers, Germany's businessmen and middle classes turned to Adolf Hitler and the Nazis to protect their interests. In January 1933 Hitler was made Chancellor (P.M.) of Germany. The rest is history!

Isolation from intervention in world affairs; protection of its own economy at the expense of trade with other countries; racial and political intolerance; unregulated growth of banking and big business; growing inequalities of wealth and poverty; a consumer led economy and stock market speculation. All of these were features of the USA in the period after 1918. All were aspects of American life which were to have a great impact not just on the USA itself in the 20th century but also on the wider world.

CHAPTER 7
Women in Britain: the start of a social revolution

1918 WAS A LANDMARK FOR WOMEN'S POLITICAL rights in Britain when, in February of that year, the Representation of the People Act granted the parliamentary vote to those women over 30 who met a property qualification. The suffragist leader, Millicent Fawcett, called it the greatest day of her life. Gaining the parliamentary vote for women was the culmination of a campaign that had begun when the MP John Stuart Mill raised the question in debates leading up to the 1867 Reform Act. The idea had been ridiculed in 1867. The focus at that time had been entirely on extending the vote to more men. By 1918, the debate was about how many women to enfranchise.

Millicent (Garrett) Fawcett (1847 to 1929)

An English feminist and leader of the non-violent suffragist movement for women's votes (NUWSS),

Millicent Fawcett was the sister of the pioneer woman doctor Elizabeth Garrett Anderson, and wife of the blind radical MP Henry Fawcett.

Change had already taken place in many other areas of women's lives before 1918, much of it due to the activities of women campaigners such as Millicent Fawcett. Married Women's Property Acts had recognized that married women were not simply a property belonging to their husband along with all their possessions, but a separate legal entity. Gone were the days when even a stolen purse would be recorded by the police as the property of the

Emmeline Pankhurst arrested, 1914

husband. Custody of Infants Acts had given mothers access to their children on separation or divorce, instead of automatically going to the husband. Matrimonial Causes Acts had also provided easier grounds for divorce.

Women had also been gaining voting rights in local political elections. In 1869 they had gained the right to vote in municipal elections. This was followed by the right to vote for school boards, for Poor Law boards and, from 1888, in County Council elections. What they had not been granted was the right to vote in parliamentary elections, even though more men had gained the vote in the 1867 and 1884 parliamentary Reform Acts.

These inconsistencies prompted women to agitate for the parliamentary vote in the years leading up to World War 1. There were two main groups of organizations. The non-violent suffragists, led by Millicent Fawcett, and the militant suffragettes, led by Emmeline Pankhurst.

Emily Davison throws herself under King George V's horse, Anmer, at the Epsom Derby June 1913

As part of the suffragette campaign, women, many of them educated and middle class, had engaged in arson, vandalism, attacks on politicians and, most famously, the sacrifice of Emily Davison in the 1913 Derby when she threw herself in front of the king's horse. To their great frustration, it was these militant actions that justified the opposition of the Liberal P.M. Asquith to giving women the parliamentary vote. How could you give the vote to people who acted so irresponsibly?

By 1918, the climate had changed and there was a sense of inevitability that some women would be given the parliamentary vote. It was once thought that this was as a reward for the contribution made by women to the war effort. In 1914, at the onset of war, Mrs. Pankhurst had called for an end to the suffragette militancy and ordered women to support the war effort. It is now thought that the major concern in 1918 was, in fact, to extend the vote to all men. Despite the franchise extensions of the 19th century, only 58% of the male population was eligible to vote, in part due to the absence of many men abroad. A Speaker's Conference had been called in 1916 to discuss extending the vote. It was agreed that the men who were risking their lives in the war must be given the vote. While there was a more positive attitude towards giving women the vote, a major concern was the fear that, if no women were enfranchised, there might be a return to the climate of pre-war suffragette militancy. Even the leader of the Anti-Suffrage League, Lord Curzon, did not want this and chose not to oppose extending the franchise to women.

The debate by 1918, therefore, was not about giving the vote to women, but about how many women should be given the vote and on what basis. Politicians were not prepared to give equal voting rights to women. The mortality rates of soldiers would have created an immediate majority of women voters if they had been granted equal voting rights.

By the Representation of the People Act, February 1918, women over 30 who were a member or married to a member of the Local Government Register (a list of those paying property taxes) or a graduate voting in a university constituency received the parliamentary vote for the first time.

This was a landmark breakthrough for women. At a stroke, some 8.4 million women gained the parliamentary vote.

As a significant percentage of the electorate, women now had to be taken into consideration by the political parties. One of the first signs of this consideration was the change in state attitudes towards prostitution, with 'tolerated brothels' in France being made out of bounds for British soldiers. Feminists ascribed their success to their newly acquired status as voters: 'Now that women have votes, things move more quickly'. (*International Women's Suffrage News* April 1918). One of the most significant changes was considered to be the Matrimonial Causes Act 1923, which made the grounds for divorce the same for men and women.

Christabel Pankhurst, daughter of Emmeline, voting in 1918 (Press Association)

133

A new phase had begun in the means by which women's groups could pressurise for changes in the law, even if, in the main, they still had to rely on the support of sympathetic male MPs.

This was only the beginning. By the Parliamentary (Qualification of Women) Act 1918, women also gained the right to be elected as MPs. Several stood in the General Election of December 1918, though only one was elected, the Sinn Fein (Irish nationalist) candidate, Countess Constance Georgina Markiewicz. She chose not to take her seat, standing as she did for Irish independence. Instead, she sat in the first Irish Dail (parliament) in Dublin.

The first woman to actually sit in the House of Commons was Nancy Astor who stood for her husband's seat of Portsmouth in 1919 when he was elevated to the House of Lords. Born in Virginia, she moved to England after her divorce from her first husband. She married Waldorf Astor in 1906. In Parliament, Astor devoted herself to the causes of women and children, temperance, education and nursery schools.

Left: Constance Markiewicz. Right: Nancy Astor

Astor had not been part of the women's suffrage movement and was dismissed by Constance Markiewicz as, 'Of the upper class, out of touch'. Though the Astor name helped her to gain the nomination, despite having six children, Nancy still had to win and hold the seat, something she was to do until 1945. She appealed to voters, including women, because of her work with Canadian soldiers, her charitable work during the war, her wit and informality. She was to prove a breath of fresh air to the Conservative party and to British politics.

With women finding it almost impossible to gain nomination for winnable seats, there was only a slow increase of women into Parliament and, eventually, into government. In 1924 Margaret Bondfield became the first woman to hold a government post, before going on to become Minister of Labour in 1929.

Women MPs in 1924. Left to Right: Dorothy Jewson; Susan Lawrence; Nancy Astor; Margaret Winteringham; Katherine Stewart-Murray; Mabel Philipson; Vera Torrington; Margaret Bondfield.

1918 brought a landmark change in women's political rights in Britain, but it did not give women equal voting rights to men. The Reform Act of that year had given the vote to all men over 21. Women had to meet both a different age qualification and a property qualification. The Act excluded many of the women who had worked in the factories and fields during the war because they were under 30. It was not only the fear of creating a majority of women voters that had caused politicians to limit the female franchise. There was a belief that, by the age of 30, most women would be married and have children, so making them less likely to endorse radical views. Voting patterns do reflect that many of the new women voters were, in fact, conservative. Some 22% of women over 30 were not even able to vote because they failed to meet the property qualification. Many of these were working class, but some were the educated middle class women who had been most prominent in the suffragette cause. Asserting their independence after the war, these women had left their parents' homes to work in white collar jobs. Living in rented accommodation, they too failed to meet the property qualification.

It was only a matter of time, however, before women gained the vote on equal terms to men. Not only did women's groups continue to campaign for an equal franchise, it was increasingly anomalous that a woman could become an MP at the age of 21 but not vote until the age of 30. The 1928 Reform Act, passed with little opposition, was to give all women over 21 the vote on equal terms to men. Women's parliamentary votes had gone from 0 to 8.4 million in 1918. After 1928 there were 15 million women voters. Millicent Fawcett wrote in her diary that she had 'the extraordinary good luck in having seen the struggle from the beginning' through to gaining the equal franchise in 1928.

Though the reasons for the low number and the role of women MPs were to remain a matter for debate throughout the 20th century, the breakthrough in 1918 was a landmark event for women's political rights. At the same time, however, women were having to fight to defend their employment rights and opportunities against the forces of regression that were operating in 1918.

Women, especially working class women, had long played a major part in the workplace, but in highly circumscribed and unequal conditions. For the main part, throughout the 19th century, they had been confined to 'traditional' women's work. The main employer was domestic service. Other major employers were factory work, laundry work, dressmaking and a range of 'sweated industries' such as chain-making.

Woman at a typewriter

Technological developments, such as the typewriter and the telephone, had brought new opportunities for female secretaries and exchange operatives in the late 19th century. Nursing had also become a respectable career for women after the reforms of Florence Nightingale.

Despite these developments, women were still considered as being unsuited to many areas of employment that we take for granted today, on account of their 'lesser strength and special health problems' (War Cabinet Committee). Additional barriers were created by the limited access that women had to higher education, as well as by attitudes about the role of married middle and upper class women: the *Angel in the House* (a popular poem by Coventry Patmore 1854).

World War 1 had challenged many of these assumptions and opened up new employment opportunities for many women, especially working class women. They had to step in to replace the thousands of men who had gone off to fight, especially after the introduction of conscription in 1916. In addition, women filled many of the new jobs created by the war. The biggest employer was in munitions, where the 'Canary Girls' were a common sight, so called because the TNT they worked with coloured their skin yellow.

Women filled many areas of employment previously considered to be 'men only'. Railway guards, bus conductors, postal workers, police, fire fighters, bank clerks. Even heavy work such as coal deliveries. Some worked on precision machinery. Many worked on the land. In total, women increased from 23.6% of the workforce in 1914 to approximately 46% by 1918. Equally striking was the increase in married women working. Nearly 40% of all women working by 1918 were married.

The needs of war did not, however, always change attitudes towards women in work. Skilled and supervisory work usually remained the domain of the men. Pay rates for women were not the equivalent of their male counterparts. Although many women were earning more than their pre-war incomes, especially if they had escaped from domestic service, the continued inequalities became a cause of friction among the female workforce. 1918 saw a landmark in women's trade union activity when women working on the buses and trams in London went on strike over wages. The strike spread to other towns in the south east of England and to the London Underground. This was one of the first equal pay strikes initiated by, led by and,

Women working in a munitions factory, 1917

ultimately, won by women. In the long history of women's employment rights, from the Match Girls' Strike of 1888 to the Equal Pay Act of 1970, a marker had been set down.

The results, however, were limited in the short term. The subsequent War Cabinet Committee report on women's wages may have promised 'equal pay for equal work', but made it clear that, even where women had replaced skilled men – itself a matter of interpretation as many skilled jobs were deemed to have been 'diluted' for women – any changes were only for the duration of the war.

The ending of the war in 1918 brought increased tensions and challenges to women's employment. In some areas, such as munitions, the demand for women workers simply disappeared. In others, the expectation was that women would give up their jobs for the returning war heroes. Any woman who tried to hold on to her job at the expense of a returning man was vilified as 'taking up an ex-serviceman's job'. Women bus and tram conductors were especially prone to being attacked by ex-servicemen.

Some 750,000 women were made redundant in 1918, with unemployment falling hardest on those who had done unskilled or semi-skilled work. This was at a time when the loss of more than 700,000 British men killed in action created a significant gender imbalance. The 1921 census showed 1,158,000 unmarried women to 919,000 men. The press talked of 'surplus women'. With no job and reduced prospects of marriage, women were eligible for Unemployment Benefit, brought in by the National Insurance Act 1911. The government, however, tried to force women back into the 'traditional' trades. The 1920 National Insurance Act stated that benefit could be refused to people who were not 'actively seeking work'. This could apply if women refused to take up available jobs in 'traditional' roles such as domestic service or laundry work.

Women who refused these pressures and continued to claim Unemployment Benefit were lambasted as 'slackers with state pay'.

New barriers were also being placed in women's path. The biggest of these was the marriage bar. Society still expected that a woman give up her work once she married. Teaching, the civil service and nursing formalized their marriage bar policies after 1918. Some companies applied it unofficially. This was in direct contradiction to the Sex Disqualification (Removal) Act of 1919 that was aimed at preventing discrimination on the grounds of gender or marriage. Even those women who defied this expectation found it impossible to continue to work once they had children. By the 1930s, only one tenth of married women worked.

Professions often grudgingly obeyed the letter of the law but found ways of negating its spirit. Women were increasingly able to train as doctors, for example, but found it difficult to obtain clinical appointments because hospitals began to restrict them to men only. Haldane's survey of women in the professions by the mid 1920's found huge discrepancies. For example, of 5,949 architects, only 21 were women. Of 7,458 Chartered Accountants, 10 were women. In the Civil Service, no woman was accepted into the administrative ranks until 1924. This was after the Committee on Recruitment in the Civil Service, set up in 1918, reported that, 'Women were apt to fall behind as the work became more responsible or complex.' In professions that had a greater proportion of women, the differences were more subtle. In teaching, most women were primary teachers and most men taught secondary. With pay scales based on the level of education that one taught, the Burnham rates of pay for teachers (1919) fixed the maximum for a woman at 4/5 the male rate. Women teachers retorted, 'No pay for Friday'.

Underlying these legal and social prejudices against women's employment opportunities post 1918 was the state of the economy. Britain emerged from World War 1 almost bankrupt and with many of its traditional markets disrupted. By 1920 the economy was moving into a deep recession, with high unemployment. Women, alongside men, were to feel the effects of this recession.

There was, however, to be no seamless return to pre-war employment patterns. Wartime experiences had changed many women for good. Country houses expressed a concern that women who had worked in munitions factories were ill-suited to domestic service. 'They know nothing of health or cleanliness, and can neither cook nor sew.' (R.Stracey, *The Cause*). Women themselves were often reluctant to return to a life of service and deference. One of the main changes for those who had escaped domestic service during the war was that their lives were no longer controlled by living-in with the employer. Mary Hewing, in *Memories of a Working Girl*, describes her sister's reluctance to work in domestic service, preferring instead to seek factory work. 'You knows when you're-a going to start work and when you're going to finish. And you gets your money on Friday'. Some employers had to find domestic staff from depressed areas such as mining districts or even in orphanages. A trend began towards 'dailies' instead of live-in staff.

New employment opportunities were also opening up for women after the war. The Education Act of 1918 raised the school leaving age to 14 for boys and girls. The Sex Disqualification (Removal) Act of 1919 made it easier for women to go to university and, ultimately, to take up professional jobs. As industry and society changed, so jobs began to open up in areas that have since become almost stereotypical women's work, for example assembly work in light industries such as making electrical goods, in the food and drink industry and in counter sales.

Social change was beginning to take place in 1918 that was to fundamentally change women's lives. In March 1918 Dr Marie Stopes published *Married Love or Love in Marriage*. It was published by the small firm of Fairfield and Co. after many of the larger publishing houses had rejected the book. Twenty thousand copies were sold in the first week and it soon went through six printings. Stopes herself predicted that the book would 'probably electrify the country'.

Dr Marie Stopes (1880 – 1958) Edinburgh-born birth control pioneer, in about 1904

World War 1 had led to freer sexual relations, but sex was still not considered a suitable topic on which to publish books. Stopes got round the risk of censorship by means of various metaphors. Her message, however, was clear. She argued that children should be planned by means of birth control, so advocating the use of contraception. Later in 1918 Stopes also wrote a birth control manual entitled *Wise Parenthood*. Three years later she founded the first birth control clinic in Britain, the Holloway Clinic. Women's lives were to be fundamentally changed. *Married Love* is the only twentieth century book to feature in Melvyn Bragg's selection of '12 books that changed the world', alongside the first folio of Shakespeare, Newton's *Principia Mathematica* and Darwin's *Origin of the Species*. It should be noted, however, that even Stopes was addressing exclusively married couples and, in the main, the 'educated middle classes'.

Younger women were also beginning to change their

Gabrielle 'Coco' Chanel (1883 – 1971)

appearance by 1918, with shorter hair and wearing shorter skirts or even trousers. The image of the 'Flapper', meaning an independent, pleasure-seeking young woman, was starting to gain ground. A *Times* article in 1918 on the problems of finding jobs for women made unemployed by the returning male workforce was entitled *The Flapper's Future*. It is no coincidence that, by 1920, the French designer Coco Chanel had introduced her 'chemise', the simple, short and loose dress that gave women freedom of movement.

Change was starting to take place in many aspects of women's lives after 1918. The appearance of many younger women was changing; divorce rates began to rocket after the Matrimonial Causes Act 1923; the birth rate began to decline as awareness of and attitudes towards contraception began to change; women made landmark advances in voting rights and increased their involvement in national politics; women gained greater access to higher education and began to demand improved access to the professions; social and economic changes began to open up new types of work for women. Commentators at the time thought that a social revolution was taking place. Though there were many obstacles and prejudices still to overcome, the story of women in the twentieth century was beginning to take shape.

CHAPTER 5
The Collapse of the Liberals:
'the funeral of a great party'

THE PERIOD LEADING UP TO WORLD WAR 1 WAS dominated by Liberal governments. In the General Election of 1906 the Liberals, one of the two great parties of Victorian politics, had won a landslide victory. Inspired by their Chancellor, David Lloyd George, they then went on to

Herbert Henry Asquith: cartoon from Vanity Fair, *1910*

introduce the radical social policies of 'New Liberalism', such as Old Age Pensions, which saw the origins of the Welfare State in twentieth century Britain.

By 1918 the Liberals were a divided party. One section, led by Lloyd George, was in a wartime coalition with the Conservatives. The other half of the Liberals, led by their former Prime Minister, Herbert Asquith, was effectively, if not officially, the main opposition party.

The Asquith Liberals were then destroyed in the General Election of 1918, winning only 28 seats. Asquith himself lost his seat. Lloyd George continued as the leader of a Conservative dominated coalition until 1922. Although the party re-united in 1923 it never recovered its pre-war identity and appeal. In 1906 the Liberals had won 399 seats. In the General Election of October 1924, the re-united party won just 40 seats. Never again would the Liberals form a majority government.

The apparently sudden collapse of the Liberal Party during and immediately after World War 1 has been the subject of much historical debate.

How had this sudden collapse come about? To what extent was it caused by World War 1? To what extent was it caused by a clash of personalities? Were there underlying causes?

At the start of the 19th century, the two main political parties were the Whigs and the Tories (Conservatives). Both were dominated by the landed aristocracy. The Whig aristocrats were distinguished from the Tories by their closer links to nonconformist (non-Anglican) Protestants and to the interests of the industrial middle classes. It had been the Whig Prime Minister, Earl Grey, who had forced through the Great Reform Act of 1832

William Ewart Gladstone: photograph by Rupert Potter

against Tory opposition which gave the vote to some of the urban middle classes.

The Liberal party had been formed in 1859 by the alliance of Whigs, 'Peelites' (former Conservatives who had supported their P.M. Sir Robert Peel in the debate on Free Trade that had split their party in the 1840s) and Radicals (those MPs who wanted more radical changes in society). Under the leadership of William Gladstone, the 'Grand Old Man' of Victorian politics, the party developed to become one of the two great political forces in Victorian Britain alongside the Conservative (or Tory) party.

In the era of Liberal ascendancy under Gladstone's leadership, the party formed four governments after 1868. It was seen as the natural party of the growing middle classes and of the newly enfranchised working classes. This link was cemented by the development of Lib-Lab candidates sponsored and endorsed by the trade unions in seats that were mainly working class.

Though they had to endure a period when mainly in opposition in the 20 years before 1906, the period leading up to World War 1 saw a resurgence and development of Liberalism. In the General Election of 1906 the Liberal Party won a landslide victory, with 399 seats to the Conservatives' 156 and, for the first time, 29 Independent Labour MPs. The party was swept back to power as the defender of the great Liberal principle of free trade between nations, seemingly threatened by the Conservative policy of tariff reform (the imposition of tariffs on imports). They were to leave their mark in this period, however, as the party that began the move towards a welfare state. In this way, the Liberals before World War 1 left a strong imprint on the social fabric of 20th century Britain.

The party's policies once in office were shaped by a growing awareness of and concern for urban poverty. Social surveys in the 1890s, such as that carried out by Charles Booth in London and by Seebohm Rowntree in York, had revealed that, in Britain's cities, almost 30% of the population were living at or below the poverty line, the minimum income needed to pay for basic necessities.

The evidence of these surveys was reinforced with the outbreak of the Second Anglo-Boer War in South Africa in 1899. Some 40% of the young men from northern industrial towns volunteering to fight to defend the Empire were rejected on health grounds, mainly because of diseases – such as rickets – caused by poverty in childhood. Under Herbert Asquith, Prime Minister from April 1908, the party embarked on a radical programmer of 'New Liberalism', carrying out a series of social reforms to help the poor, the aged and the disadvantaged that have been called the 'Birth of the Welfare State'.

Most prominent of their reforms were the introduction of Old Age Pensions (1908); National Insurance against sickness and unemployment (1911) and the 'People's Budget' (1909) with its emphasis on taxing the wealthy in order to pay for the social reforms that benefited the poor. In response to the opposition of the Conservative dominated House of Lords, the Liberals passed the Parliament Act 1911. No longer were the Lords able to

A York slum from images collected by Rowntree, 1901.

prevent the passage of 'money bills' and were only able to delay other legislation passed by the House of Commons for a maximum of two years.

The dominant political personality driving New Liberalism and the 'scourge' of the privileged classes was the Chancellor, David Lloyd George. The Prime Minister and his Chancellor had very different backgrounds and personalities. Asquith was a graduate of Balliol College, Oxford and had a high society wife. Lloyd George was a Welsh speaking Baptist, brought up in a shoe-maker's home, who never went to university. It was said that Asquith told everything to his wife while Lloyd George told everything to other people's wives!

1906 to 1914 was the high water mark of New Liberalism. It was, however, to prove a false dawn in Liberal fortunes. By 1918 the Liberals were a divided and broken party, never again to form a majority government.

Lloyd George with Winston Churchill in 1907

Historians disagree about the importance of World War 1 in causing the collapse of the Liberals. In 1934, George Dangerfield, in *The Strange Death of Liberal England* argued that the party was already in terminal decline before 1914. This view was later challenged. Trevor Wilson in *The Downfall of the Liberal Party* (1966) argued that the

Liberals were like an ageing man in 1914, already unwell, but who was then finished off by being knocked over by a bus in the form of World War 1. More recently, historians have been stressing how well the Liberals coped with the challenges that they faced up to 1914 and how limited Labour was as a force within parliament at that time. Certainly, Labour were in no position to form a government or even the main opposition party before 1914. Kenneth Morgan, in *The new Liberal party from dawn to downfall 1906-24* states that, '... the Liberals were destroyed by the First World War. They almost disintegrated as a party.'

The outbreak of World War 1 makes any analysis of pre-war political trends uncertain. What is not in doubt is that the war was to test Liberal principles and to split the party in two.

The outbreak of war was a potential challenge to Liberal unity, given that they were the traditional anti-war party. Calls by the Liberal Association (a national Liberal organisation) for a resolution of neutrality in the days before war was declared were, however, swept away by the German invasion of Belgium. Asquith and his Foreign Secretary, Grey, were able to convince the

Front page of The Times, *5 August 1914*

country and their colleagues that the war was a necessary evil imposed on the government by the Germans.

In the event, only two Cabinet ministers had resigned in opposition to military involvement in Europe. What created the tensions within the party, however, was the long duration of the war and the pressures caused by failures.

The demands of waging total war necessarily brought the need for increased state interference and control, something which clashed with the Liberal principles and beliefs in safeguarding individual civil liberties. This was seen in the passing of the Defence of the Realm Act (DORA) by the Liberal government in 1914. Re-enacted several times during the war, it was to give the state increasing powers to restrict and control lives, such as censorship of the press, rationing, licensing laws and control over manufacturing.

At the same time, there were growing questions as to the ability of Asquith and the Liberals to successfully wage a total war.

Winston Churchill with the Naval Wing of the Royal Flying Corps, 1914

The crisis came in 1915 to 1916. First there was the scandal of the 'shells shortage'. Then came the failure of the Gallipoli campaign (April 1915 to January 1916). This was Winston Churchill's plan to attack the 'weak underbelly' of the Central Powers in Turkey, opening up a new front that would draw German troops away from the Western Front and providing a supply route to our ally, Russia. The campaign was a military disaster. The resignation of Admiral Fisher as First Sea Lord on 15 May 1915 was interpreted as a sign of his growing frustration at working with the government and as a direct criticism of Churchill's plan.

The Gallipoli campaign. A failed attempt to integrate naval and land attacks in the Dardanelles.

The growing pressures and criticisms prompted Asquith to form a coalition with the Conservatives and some Labour MPs in May 1915 rather than face a wartime election. This, however, only served to paper over the widening cracks.

Though he became Minister of Munitions, Lloyd George began to side more and more with the Conservative leader, Bonar Law, in the need for a more dynamic prosecution of the war.

A decisive issue was the argument in the winter of 1915-16 over the need to replace voluntary enlistment with conscription. Many Liberals saw conscription as a betrayal of Liberal principles. The Home Secretary, John Simon, resigned on principle.

Asquith had reluctantly accepted the need for conscription to replace voluntary enlistment, passing the Military Enlistment Act in January 1916. Lloyd George's threat to resign then forced him to accept the inclusion of married men as conscripts in May 1916.

Left: Andrew Bonar Law, Canadian-born Conservative leader and Prime Minister in 1923
Right: John Simon. Liberal politician who was one of only three people to serve as Home Secretary, Foreign Secretary and Chancellor of the Exchequer.

The failure of the Somme offensive in July 1916 added to Lloyd George's frustrations with Asquith's war leadership. In December 1916, supported by Bonar Law and the Conservatives, Lloyd George proposed the creation of a small, executive 'War Committee', sometimes referred to as a War Cabinet, with himself as chairman. Asquith, though Prime Minister, would be left responsible only for domestic matters and would not be a member of this new committee. It was this development that led to Asquith's resignation.

The actual sequence of events by which Lloyd George replaced Asquith is still the subject of historical debate, especially regarding Lloyd George's political ambitions. J.M. McEwen's *Lloyd George versus Asquith December 1916* describes how the circumstances are surrounded by 'talk of intrigue and conspiracy'.

On 3 December 1916, Asquith and Lloyd George had met to discuss the idea of a War Cabinet. At this meeting, Asquith was willing to consider the plan. The next day, 4 December, Asquith was ridiculed in the 'Northcliffe article' that appeared in *The Times*. Lord Northcliffe was a newspaper and publishing magnate who

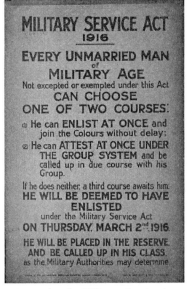

Poster for the Military Service Act 1916 (Conscription)

155

owned, among other papers, *The Times* and the *Daily Mail*. His press had consistently criticised Asquith's handling of the war. The article, probably written by Geoffrey Robinson, but with Northcliffe's approval, described how Asquith was to be reduced to a 'figurehead' status. Believing that Lloyd George was behind the article, Asquith resigned. It is possible that Asquith expected to be called back by both Liberals and Conservatives, so securing his position. In the event, after consulting Bonar Law, it was Lloyd George who was asked by the king to form a new government. Lloyd George went ahead and formed a coalition government with Conservative support, some Labour support and the support of approximately 100 Liberals.

Lloyd George stated that he wanted to avoid any 'organic division' of the Liberal Party and hoped that it could reassert itself as a unified and distinctive political movement once the war was over. At first, the Liberals who remained loyal to Asquith, or 'Squiffites' as they were known, were not officially an opposition party, even though they sat on the opposition benches. They even kept up a single whip system, albeit using two men. The division, however, between those Liberals who supported the coalition government of David Lloyd George and those who were still loyal to Asquith, became increasingly bitter. The 'Squiffites' could not forgive what they saw as the betrayal of Asquith by Lloyd George. This was most clearly seen in the Maurice debate of 1918 when 98 Asquith Liberals voted against the government, whom they accused of misleading the House of Commons over troop numbers in France. Historians see this vote as a landmark in the Liberal split.

This division continued after the ending of the war. Lloyd George had invited Asquith and his Liberal supporters to re-join the government in time for the planned General Election in December 1918. Asquith refused, wanting nothing less than the position of Prime Minister. Lloyd George was forced to organise his own 'coalition' Liberal party and negotiate an electoral pact with the Conservatives. Hence the name of the 'Coupon Election' after the 'coupons' given to pro-Lloyd George Liberals to ensure they were not challenged by Conservative candidates and vice versa. With Lloyd George seen as the 'Man who won the war', the Conservative-Liberal alliance won 506 seats. It was, however, mainly a Conservative government. The Lloyd George 'Coalition' Liberals won 133 seats. Asquith's Liberals won only 28 seats and Asquith himself was defeated in his seat of East Fife. Winston Churchill, at that time a Liberal member of the coalition government, commented, 'Here is a great split'.

Lloyd George continued to assert his Liberal principles from within the coalition government. 'I am still a Liberal. Look at what I am doing: we are promoting housing, promoting health policies; we have got money extending unemployment insurance.' These assertions of Liberal principles were, however, weakened by the government's association with the Treaty of Versailles that many Liberals saw as vindictive because of Keynes' criticisms in his book *The Economic Consequences of the Peace* (1919). It was also associated with the policy of repression and reprisals carried out by the 'Black and Tans' in Ireland.

Never again would the Liberal Party be able to form a majority government and shape the agenda of British politics as it had done before 1914. When, in October 1922, the Conservatives voted to end the coalition with Lloyd George, the Liberals contested the 1922 General Election as two distinct parties. The Asquith Liberals won 62 seats and Lloyd George's Liberals won 53 seats. Though it re-united in 1923 over Free Trade, the party never managed to re-establish its identity and appeal to the British voters, caught as it now was between the tide of Conservatism and the rise of Labour. The nadir came in the General Election of October 1924, in which the re-united Liberals won just 40 seats.

The timing of the Liberal collapse is clear. What is more open to debate is the underlying cause. Though World War 1 was undoubtedly a catalyst, some would point to the longer term social, economic and political changes taking place in Britain that weakened the appeal of Liberalism. It is also open to debate as to how united the Liberal Party was, even before the split during World War 1.

The 1906 General Election had perhaps masked the growing problems facing the Liberals. It was to be the last election in which the Liberals won an overall majority in the House of Commons. Already, they were being challenged by the move of middle class votes towards the Conservatives and by the militant brand of 'new unionism' that thought Labour should take a more independent political stance.

A significant factor was the growing industrialism of Britain and the rise of an enfranchised and organized working class, at first through trade unions and then in politics. Initially, the new working class voters, enfranchised in 1867 and 1884, had tended to vote Liberal. Increasingly, however, the militant 'new unionism' began to clamor for a separate political stance for the working classes. In 1893 Keir Hardie formed the Independent Labour Party (ILP).

Keir Hardie

In the years before World War 1, the ILP operated within parliament as the allies of the Liberals, but the rise of Labour was also a threat to the Liberals. It was partly because of this threat that Lloyd George had promoted the social welfare policies of New Liberalism, in an attempt to safeguard working class support for his party rather than lose it to the Labour Party. The Liberal move to the left in its social policies risked, however, alienating middle class

159

voters who faced increased taxes and whose fears were encouraged by a barrage of Conservative propaganda.

An editorial in the pro-Conservative *Daily Mail*, 30 April 1909, stated, 'The budget which Mr. Lloyd George laid before the House of Commons yesterday is admirably calculated to harass every class of businessman. We have to admit that the Budget resembles the production of wild Socialists, not a Cabinet of sober and thoughtful business-men. The middle class and the income tax paying class in particular are singled out for special and cruel attack.'

At the same time, the Liberals' alliance with Labour was becoming more strained by the growing tide of indus-trial unrest throughout Britain in the years leading up to 1914. After a period of intense industrial unrest beginning in July 1910, the three largest trade unions – the Miners,

Poster complaining about Lloyd George's taxation policies

the Railwaymen and Transport Workers – had formed a triple alliance in early 1914. Talk of an impending General Strike was only ended by the outbreak of World War 1. The ILP's close links with the trade union movement inevitably placed a great strain on their alliance with the Liberals.

With middle class fears of Liberal social welfare policies being fanned by the media and the Lib-Lab pact also growing more strained because of industrial unrest, the Liberals were facing challenges from the right and left of British politics leading up to 1914. In addition, they came under growing pressure from other factors.

The circumstances of the 1906 General Election had been unusual because of the widespread hostility to Conservative plans for Tariff Reform that threatened Free Trade. After almost twenty years spent mainly out of office, the issue revived one of the great principles of the Liberal Party and hence their popularity with the electorate. It was the only election after 1885 in which the Liberals won a majority of English constituencies. They also benefited from the electoral system, winning 59.6% of the seats with only 49.4% of the votes. By the time of the 1910 General Election the Liberals had already lost their overall parliamentary majority as Lloyd George's reforms began to alarm the middle class voters.

They were forced to rely on the support of Irish Nationalist MPs in parliament but their pursuit of Irish Home Rule in return for this support only triggered the Ulster Rebellion and strengthened opposition to the Liberals. The party also suffered from the inability of Asquith to deal with the issue of women's suffrage. The Liberals would have lost male support had they endorsed votes for women, but, at the same time, Asquith's opposition weakened the party's Liberal credentials. In by-elections between 1911 and 1914 the Conservatives gained 15 seats from the Liberals.

Then came the test of Liberal principles and unity posed by World War 1. 'By 1918, all the key Liberal principles had been compromised' (Dr Michael Lynch *The Liberals and the Great War 1914-18*). Entry into the war had compromised the notion of the Liberals as a peace party. The economic regulations of the state had ended free trade. Conscription and censorship had challenged the Liberal concept of individual freedom of choice.

If World War 1 widened the divisions in the Liberal party and helped to bring about its downfall, the war had speeded up the rise of Labour. Initially, Labour had also been split by entry into the war when some Lib-Lab MPs such as Ramsay MacDonald resigned. Labour did benefit, however, from the inclusion of some of their MPs in the wartime Coalition government. Their leader, Arthur Henderson, became the first Labour Cabinet Minister when he joined Asquith's coalition in 1915. He was joined by two other Labour Ministers in Lloyd George's Cabinet, before resigning in August 1917 over policy differences.

The General Election of December 1918 took place in a very different climate to politics before the war. Labour had emerged as a united and distinct political party based on socialist principles. When invited to join the post-war coalition government, George Bernard Shaw had advised the Labour Party Conference to tell Lloyd George, 'Nothing doing.' With the Liberals divided, Labour was now the clear alternative voice in British politics. In 1918, the party adopted a new constitution and published a manifesto, *Labour and the New Social Order*. Clause IV of the constitution committed Labour to a socialist agenda based on common ownership of the means of production. Labour won 63 seats in the 1918 General Election and then 142 seats in 1922.

The rise of Labour took place in a changing political landscape after World War 1. The 1918 Reform Act had tripled the electorate, including most women over 30 and all men over 21. Many of the new male voters were return-ing working class soldiers, with a natural sympathy for Labour. Many of the new female voters were to support the Conservatives. Alongside these electoral differences, Irish Nationalist support for the Liberals had collapsed after the Easter Rising of 1916 in Dublin and then been pushed aside by the rise of Sinn Fein, who wanted Irish independ-ence and nothing to do with Westminster.

Rapidly becoming the 'third party' in British politics, the Liberals found it difficult to position themselves on the spectrum of left-right politics while defining its distinctive appeal to a widening electorate. In 1923 to 1924 Ramsay MacDonald led a minority Labour government, the first Labour government in British political history and a sign of the changing political landscape. The Liberals backed the minority government in the hope of rebuilding its former progressive alliance, but Labour was not willing to co-oper-ate. The Liberals then withdrew their support for the minority Labour government.

In the ensuing General Election of October 1924, the unified Liberal party gained just 40 seats. Labour's Sidney Webb called it, 'The funeral of a great party'. The

Ramsay Macdonald and Arthur Henderson on a state visit to Berlin

163

Liberals have spent the years since then trying to establish their distinct identity in British politics and, at the same time, their relationship with the Conservative and Labour parties, both within and out of government.

CHAPTER 9
Ireland divided: independence and civil war

THE YEARS IMMEDIATELY FOLLOWING 1918 SAW the culmination of a long and bitter struggle by the Irish to regain their independence from England. It was a struggle that had been growing in intensity in the years leading up to World War 1, a period during which the problem of Ireland had been at the centre of British politics.

Reliant on the support of Irish MPs to retain a majority at Westminster, the Liberal Government had introduced an Irish Home Rule Bill in April 1912, by which Ireland would have been given its own parliament within the United Kingdom. Due to become law in September 1914 under the terms of the Parliament Act, the Home Rule Bill had triggered the threat of a civil war in Ireland because the Protestant majority of Ulster (Northern Ireland) rejected the prospect of government by a majority Roman Catholic Irish parliament. Only the outbreak of World War 1 in August 1914 had averted an Irish civil war by postponing the implementation of Home Rule. The postponement, however, frustrated hard-line Irish nationalists. In 1916, in a bid to seize independence, this group began the Easter Rising in Dublin. The Rising was soon crushed by British forces, but the harsh repression that followed it only fuelled the growth of Irish nationalism.

At the start of 1918 the whole of Ireland still remained a part of the United Kingdom, represented in Westminster by Irish MPs and subject to the authority of the British government and crown. This political situation was, however, highly unstable. Actions and events between 1918 and 1923 were to transform Ireland and to shape its history since.

In the aftermath of World War 1, Ireland endured firstly a War of Independence (1919 to 1921) that brought about the division of Ireland between the mainly Catholic Irish Free State in the South and the mainly Protestant Northern Ireland. It then endured the even more violent Civil War (1922 to 1923) in the South between the Nationalists, who grudgingly accepted a degree of self-government from Britain as a first step towards freedom, and the Republicans who wanted full independence immediately.

The roots of the violence and instability in the period 1918 to 1923 can be traced back earlier in Ireland's history.

The Act of Union of 1801 that merged the separate kingdoms of Ireland and Great Britain and abolished the Irish Parliament had been imposed on the Irish because of British concerns about national security during the Napoleonic wars with France. The fear was that the French would use the mainly Catholic Ireland as a base from which to attack England. Henceforth, Ireland would be governed from Westminster and represented by Irish MPs elected to the British Parliament.

Carried out against the wishes of many Irish, union with England was challenged throughout the 19th century by Irish nationalist groups such as the Fenians, often through violence.

The Liberal Prime Minister, William Gladstone, introduces the Home Rule Bill for Ireland, 1886

In the late 19th century, the Liberal leader, William Gladstone, made it his 'mission to pacify Ireland' by granting Home Rule. By Home Rule, Ireland would have its own parliament to govern Irish affairs but would still come under the overall authority of Westminster.

It was a solution to the Irish problem that was opposed by the Conservative party and by a section of Gladstone's own party, the Liberal Unionists. They saw Home Rule as a first step in the breaking up of the United Kingdom. In 1886 the Liberal Unionists split with Gladstone to form a political alliance with the Conservatives in opposition to Irish Home Rule. A complete merger followed in 1912, creating the Conservative and Unionist Party.

It was also a solution that not all Irish nationalists agreed with. Home Rule effectively offered devolution within the United Kingdom. Ireland would have its own parliament to govern its own affairs, but would still come under the overall authority of Westminster and retain the British

167

monarch as Head of State. Attitudes in Ireland towards such a limited independence had always been divided. Some nationalists, such as Daniel O'Connell in the 1830s and 1840s had wanted separatism through a complete repeal of the Act of Union. These views are refered to as Irish republicanism, the demand for a completely independent republic of Ireland. Others, such as Isaac Butt, had accepted the prospect of Home Rule within the UK, seeing a Dublin Parliament as the 'promised land' that would right old wrongs.

Gladstone's First Home Rule Bill in 1886 was defeated in the House of Commons. His Second Bill was defeated in 1893 by the Conservative and Unionist majority in the House of Lords.

Isaac Butt, the moderate leader of the Irish Home Rule Party: a cartoon from Vanity Fair*, 1873.*

Ireland had split the Liberal party and so contributed to their years in opposition before 1905. In the General Election of that year the Liberals returned to power with a large majority. Their leader, Herbert Asquith, was, however, not as keen as Gladstone had been to introduce a Home Rule Bill. By 1905, the party had other, more pressing, priorities, such as the welfare reforms of New Liberalism.

Prime Minister Asquith (second from left) visiting Ireland during the troubles over Home Rule, 1914.

This was to change after the 1910 General Election. The Liberals lost their overall majority in the House of Commons and were forced to rely on the support of the Irish Parliamentary Party (IPP), traditionally known as the Home Rule Party, to stay in power. The price for this support was another Home Rule Bill. There still remained, however, the obstacle of the Conservative majority in the House of Lords. John Redmond, the leader of the Irish Parliamentary Party, stated in 1910 that the Lords' veto alone stood between Ireland and a successful Home Rule Bill. The solution, supported by Redmond, was to force through the Parliament Act of 1911. The House of Lords could henceforth only delay a Bill passed by the Commons for a maximum of two years, not defeat it. The exception was any Finance Bill, which it had no power to delay.

John Redmond, leader of the Irish Parliamentary Party, addresses an audience

The Third Home Rule Bill was introduced in April 1912. It would give a devolution of power to Ireland rather than full independence. Purely Irish questions would be dealt with by an Irish Parliament. The British Parliament in Westminster would still include Irish members and would deal with all issues relating to the crown, the army and navy, foreign policy and customs.

By now, however, there was an added complication. The Protestant majority of Ulster were not prepared to be governed by an Irish parliament which they felt would neglect and harm Ulster's economic, social and religious interests. Led by Edward Carson, the Protestants of Ulster believed that Home Rule meant Rome rule, because they would be a minority in a united Ireland.

Encouraged by the Conservatives and Unionists, Carson vowed that, 'Ulster will fight and Ulster will be right'. A novel of 1914 entitled *The North Afire* envisaged a violent civil war between Nationalists and Loyalists in Ulster. Even some English Unionists, such as George Wyndham, thought that Liberal attempts to pass Home Rule should be met by violence, with the aid of the Army, the Navy and the Territorials to prevent constitutional change.

Attitudes in the South towards Home Rule remained divided, but were mostly in favor. Arthur Griffith, leader of the Irish republican party, Sinn Fein (We Ourselves), founded in 1905, at first denounced the 1912 Bill as a 'grotesque abortion' of their demands. Then he began to rally the republicans (those wanting full separation of Ireland from the United Kingdom) to prepare to become the main party within an Irish Parliament. Those who thought that Home Rule was totally inadequate were, at this stage, a small minority.

A protest rally against Home Rule in Belfast, 1914

As the clock ticked down towards the legalizing of the Home Rule Bill under the terms of the Parliament Act, so the tensions rose. Asquith was sensitive to the need to compromise if civil war in Ireland was to be averted. In a letter to Winston Churchill, he wrote, 'I always thought that, in the end, we should probably have to make some sort of bargain about Ulster as the price of Home Rule'. Carson and James Craig, meanwhile, organized the signing of the Ulster Covenant against the 'coercion of Ireland'. In January 1913 various Protestant groups, such as the Orangemen, were organized into the Ulster Volunteers. Armed and drilled, they prepared to fight.

Edward Carson inspects his Ulster Volunteers, 1914

The South also began to arm itself and formed the Irish Volunteers to defend their cause.

With civil war in Ireland looming, the Home Rule Bill received the Royal Assent under the terms of the Parliament Act on 18 September 1914. Weeks before, however, World War 1 had broken out and the Act was immediately suspended for the duration of hostilities.

John Redmond persuades Irish nationals to volunteer

Redmond accepted this delay, seeing Germany as the greater threat. Many of the Irish Volunteers followed Redmond's urge to support the war effort and enlisted in Kitchener's Army. A core of republicans were not prepared to wait. Directed by the Irish Republican Brotherhood and commanded by men such as James Connolly, Patrick Pearse and Eamon de Valera, they refused to follow Redmond's lead. These men staged the Easter Rising in Dublin 1916, in an attempt to force the granting of independence. Key locations were seized, most notably the Dublin Post Office, and an Irish Republic proclaimed.

The shattered remains of the General Post Office in Sackville Street, Dublin, after the Easter Rising.

The Rising was put down within a week and was even condemned by many in Ireland itself, often because members of their families were fighting against the Germans in the British Army. Arrested Volunteers were hissed at, pelted with refuse and denounced as murderers as they were marched under escort after the Rising. Attitudes began to change, however, when the British government badly mishandled the aftermath of the Rising. Ninety were sentenced to death by court martial, with 15 sentences confirmed. The execution of the leaders in Kilmainham Goal aroused great sympathy. None more so than Connolly, taken out and shot while tied to a chair because his shattered ankle meant he was unable to walk to his death. Another death that touched the Irish imagination was that of Joseph Plunkett, who married his sweetheart,

Grace Gifford, in Kilmainham Goal immediately prior to being executed there on 4 May 1916.

James Connolly's gravestone

The only commandant of the Easter Rising not to be executed was Eatmon de Valera. The reasons why have been much debated. His exemption was probably due to a combination of factors but one was certainly that the American Consulate made representations on his behalf. De Valera had been born in New York City and it was not clear whether or not he was an American citizen. Britain did not want to risk antagonizing the USA by executing somebody who was possibly an American citizen just when it was endeavoring to get the USA to enter World War 1 on the Allied side.

The execution of the leaders of the Rising and the arrest of over 3,000 political activists began to turn public opinion in the South of Ireland towards the republican cause. In April 1917 a broad political movement was formed under the banner of Sinn Fein, which soon began to oust the

Irish Parliamentary Party in gaining popular support in the South of Ireland. In 1917, Sinn Fein stated that its aims were, 'securing the international recognition of Ireland as an independent Irish Republic'.

In this, it was helped by the policies of the British government.

In a bid to start negotiations over the implementation of Home Rule, the British government released prisoners arrested after the Easter Rising. Ulster Unionist opposition, however, ensured the failure of any attempts to move towards a political settlement and many of the released prisoners simply joined the Sinn Fein campaign.

Attitudes hardened in the last year of World War 1. Riots and confrontations began to develop between political campaigners in the South and the Royal Irish Constabulary. Several hundred were arrested under charges of conspiring with Germany. Others were detained under legislation banning public parades. Then came the conscription crisis.

Because of the manpower shortage on the Western Front in the face of the German Spring Offensive of 1918, the British Government attempted to extend conscription to the whole of Ireland. This was fiercely opposed in the South of Ireland and caused a big swing towards Sinn Fein and the nationalist cause.

In the General Election of December 1918 Sinn Fein won 73 of the 105 Irish seats in Westminster, the main exceptions being in Ulster. Their ranks included the first woman MP elected to Westminster, Constance Markiewicz (page 134). She fought against British rule in the Easter Rising 1916 when she famously kissed her revolver before handing it over to a British officer at the point of surrender. Markiewicz was the only woman involved in the Rising to be court-martialled and sentenced to death, a sentence commuted to life imprisonment on account of her gender. Freed in a general amnesty, Markiewicz became the first British female MP in 1918 when elected as Member of Parliament for Sinn Fein. She refused her seat and, instead, served as Minister of Labour in the first Irish Dail (parliament). Markiewicz bitterly opposed the Anglo-Irish Treaty that accepted limited home rule in December 1921 and supported the Republican forces in the Civil War. She joined de Valera's Fianna Fail party in 1926, before dying in 1927.

Sinn Fein benefited from the widening of the electorate throughout the United Kingdom under the 1918 Reform Act. The measure, designed to enfranchise the returning soldiers and give some recognition to women's campaign for the vote, had the unintended effect of creating a new generation of voters in Ireland. Inspired by stories of the Easter Rising and holding no historic allegiance to the IPP, many of the new voters in the South of Ireland voted for Sinn Fein in the 1918 General Election. Sinn Fein had also been wrongly blamed by the British government for the Easter Rising, even though they had played no part in it, so gaining them sympathy. Since then, the party had gained credit for leading the opposition in Ireland to the extension of conscription.

The Sinn Fein MPs refused to take up their seats at Westminster or to wait on the British government finding a solution to Ulster opposition. In January 1919, 30 Sinn Fein MPs met in Dublin to proclaim the first Dail, an independent parliament of the Irish Republic. Many other elected members were unable to attend because they were still imprisoned. 'Absent, imprisoned by foreigners,' as the roll call put it. With de Valera as its president, the Dail ratified the Declaration of the Republic made during the 1916 Easter Rising. It was an open statement of rejection and rebellion against Westminster.

The same day as the Dail was proclaimed, the Irish War of Independence began with the Soloheadbeg ambush of a gelignite transport in which two policemen were killed.

Republican attacks were coordinated by Michael Collins, Director of Intelligence for the Volunteers or IRA. The Irish Republican Army (IRA) was formed in 1917 from those Irish Volunteers who refused to enlist in the British Army. Others were later to join it who had been British soldiers. As the War of Independence gathered force, so the IRA grew in power and authority. Though the IRA was nominally subordinate to the Dail, the latter was hampered by a ban on it imposed by Britain. In September 1919, the British Government had declared the Dail to be an illegal assembly since Ireland was still a part of the United Kingdom. In April 1921 the Dail declared the IRA to be the legitimate army of the Irish Republic.

A 'squad' was created to assassinate the detectives who were arresting Republican activists and an attempt was made to kill John French, the Lord Lieutenant of Ireland. Violence was reinforced by civil disobedience, such as the refusal of railway workers to transport British troops.

By 1920, a series of attacks on rural police stations by IRA units saw the Royal Irish Constabulary withdraw to fortified barracks in towns. Sinn Fein began to take over the functions of government in rural areas, such as tax collection and law enforcement.

Lloyd George responded with a carrot and stick approach. The stick was the creation of the Black and Tans, a force of paramilitary police created mainly from war veterans. The force was the brainchild of Winston Churchill. Officially the Royal Irish Constabulary Reserve Force, their nickname came from the mixed uniforms that they initially wore, a mixture of British Army khaki (tan coloured)and RIC rifle green (almost black). The name soon became synonymous with attacks on Irish civilians and property in response to IRA attacks.

Black and Tans outside a pub

Reprisals on Irish civilians for IRA attacks brought a grave escalation of the violence. A climax was reached on Bloody Sunday, 21 November 1920. Units of Collins' squad launched an attack on British intelligence officers, killing 12 officers and two auxiliary policemen in a series of raids. British forces then shot and killed 14 civilians, with 16 more wounded, at a Gaelic football match in Dublin's Croke Park. Both at the time and in recently available records of the official British military enquiry, the British authorities claimed that the troops were first fired upon by unknown civilians in the crowd when they arrived to carry out a controlled search. The troops fired back, though the enquiry stated that they did so without orders and in an indiscriminate manner. This is at odds with the accounts of 30 Irish survivors of the massacre who claimed that the British troops fired first. That same evening, two high ranking Dublin IRA officers were killed. In all, 30 people died on Bloody Sunday, 21 November 1920.

Meanwhile, Britain went ahead with attempts to introduce the Fourth Home Rule Bill, but with changes that recognized the developments in Ireland. Influenced by the Walter Long Committee, the Government of Ireland Act 1920 offered a firm division of Ireland into the North and the South, each with their own parliament. The parliament of Northern Ireland met for the first time on 22 June 1921.

The South did not want to accept such a restricted freedom but, with no end to the violence in sight, a truce was declared between Irish Republican forces and the British Government on 11 July 1921 to allow talks on a political settlement. In December 1921 an Irish delegation led by Michael Collins and Arthur Griffith signed the Anglo-Irish Treaty that recognized the creation of the Irish Free State, later to become the Republic of Ireland.

The Irish Free State was to comprise only 26 of the 32 counties of Ireland because the Anglo-Irish Treaty allowed the six counties of Ulster to opt out if they wished to and return to the United Kingdom. They did so immediately, effectively confirming the division of Ireland envisaged in the Government of Ireland Act of 1920 and the separate existence of Northern Ireland.

Though given full authority by de Valera to negotiate with the British, acceptance of the Anglo-Irish Treaty by Collins and Griffith was to split the southern Irish ranks and lead to the bitter and bloody Civil War. This was fought between the forces of the Irish Free State (the Nationalists), supported and heavily armed by the British Government, and the Republicans. Lasting from June 1922 to May 1923, the Civil War caused more Irish casualties than the War of Independence and left Irish society divided for generations.

The Republicans opposed many features of the Anglo-Irish Treaty. They saw it as a betrayal of the Irish Republic and deemed it to be the creation of British imperialism. Sinn Fein had won the 1918 General Election in the South on a promise of breaking away from the British crown, the Westminster parliament and the British Empire, rejecting

Arthur Griffith during the peace conference leading to the Anglo-Irish Treaty, December 1921.

previous offers of Home Rule. The terms of the Anglo-Irish Treaty fell far short of the full independence that they sought. The Irish Free State would be an autonomous dominion within the British Empire, similar to Australia and Canada. Its head of state would be the British monarch, to whom members of the Irish parliament would have to swear the Oath of Allegiance. Britain would also retain three 'treaty ports' on the south coast of Ireland, occupied by the Royal Navy. Not least, it recognized the division of Ireland by allowing the counties of Ulster to opt out of the treaty.

Others in the South, such as Collins, reluctantly accepted the Anglo-Irish Treaty as giving the 'freedom to achieve freedom'. In any case, he and Griffith had ultimately been given two hours by Lloyd George to accept the treaty or face the renewal of 'immediate and terrible war'.

Michael Collins addresses the crowd to argue for the Anglo-Irish Treaty, 1922

The Dail narrowly voted in favor of accepting the Anglo-Irish Treaty by 64 votes to 57 in January 1922 but the majority vote was rejected by the Republicans, such as de Valera. He said that supporters of the Anglo-Irish Treaty 'broke their oath to the Irish republic'. De Valera resigned as President of the Republic. When the pro-treaty side narrowly won the General

Election of June 1922, de Valera said that, 'The majority have no right to do wrong'.

Political divisions soon turned to violence. Most crucial in causing this was the split in IRA ranks. In March 1922 the IRA called a convention in which a majority repudiated the right of the Dail to dissolve the Republic after it had been declared in 1918. The anti-treaty majority of the IRA formed their own 'Army Executive' which they declared to be the true government of the country. In April 1922 they seized control of the Four Courts, the main legal centre of Dublin. Attempts by Collins to agree a compromise that would avoid bloodshed were vetoed by the British Government. Collins negotiated a pact with de Valera to form a joint government of pro and anti-treaty members. It was Winston Churchill who was most vociferous in his opposition to this during Cabinet debates, saying that any such compromise would undermine the Anglo-Irish Treaty. He insisted that the Provisional Government, set up to oversee the transition towards the Irish Free State, act to regain control of the Four Courts or British troops would intervene.

Ireland descended into a civil war. De Valera, though at heart wanting a political and not a military solution, warned in a speech that, if the Anglo-Irish Treaty were accepted, the fight for freedom would still go on, and the Irish people, instead of fighting foreign soldiers, would have to fight the Irish soldiers of an Irish government set up by Irishmen. A few days later, in another speech, de Valera strengthened the warning, stating that the IRA would have to, 'Wade through the blood of the soldiers of the Irish Government, and perhaps through that of some members of the Irish Government to get their freedom'. When the speech was reported in the Irish Independent, de Valera accepted the accuracy of the report, but deplored that it had been published.

Violence began with the assassination in London of Field-Marshal Sir Henry Wilson, a retired British General who had been involved in British Intelligence during the War of Independence and acted as security adviser for the newly created Northern Ireland. Even this event is cloaked in controversy. It was never proven that it was carried out on the orders of the anti-treaty IRA. It has even been claimed that the two men who killed Wilson may have done so with the approval and help of Collins himself. The two assailants, Joseph O'Sullivan and Reginald Dunne, both 24 and members of the London Brigade of the IRA, would admit only that they had shot Wilson. Ironically, both had been born in London, whereas Wilson had been born in Ireland into a unionist family. Both assailants had also served in the British Army during WW1. O'Sullivan had lost a leg at the Battle of Ypres. His wooden leg had hampered his attempts to flee after the execution of Wilson. Instead of fleeing the scene himself, Dunne had remained to try and aid O'Sullivan. Both were hanged in Wandsworth Prison on 10 August 1922.

Whoever was to blame, the death of Wilson was the spark that began the Irish Civil War. The British Government blamed the anti-treaty IRA and insisted that Collins immediately crush the IRA base in the Four Courts. Collins borrowed two 18 pounder artillery guns from the British and bombarded the Four Courts until the anti-treaty garrison surrendered. Violence immediately spread to other parts of Dublin and throughout Ireland.

The pro-treaty forces of the Provisional Government, led by Michael Collins, were able to take Dublin and the cities of the South thanks to British supplies of vehicles, equipment and, especially, artillery. The anti-treaty IRA were forced to turn to guerrilla warfare.

The South became embroiled in a spiral of increasing violence on both sides.

In August 1922, Collins, head of the Provisional Government and Commander-in-Chief of the National Army, was killed in an ambush by the anti-treaty IRA whilst visiting his native Cork. Instead of taking shelter in his armoured car, or simply driving away when the convoy was ambushed, Collins, for some unknown reason, chose to stop and fire back himself from behind an ordinary car. He was killed by a single shot. Denis O'Neill, the IRA man credited with killing Collins, had been a trained marksman in the British Army during WW1. He was later to receive a state pension for his actions.

The coffin of Michael Collins, leader of the Free State Forces, being driven through the streets of Dublin, August 1922.

The government responded with a series of executions of captured Republicans. The IRA responded in turn with their own assassinations, such as of the pro-treaty MP Sean Hales, and four other pro-treaty IRA leaders. The violence was not confined to political activists and those directly involved in the armed conflict. Gemma Clark's *Everyday Violence in the Irish Civil War* (2014) describes a violent undercurrent as authority in many areas went into meltdown and local enmities were given free rein. One notable feature was the burning by the IRA of many 'big houses'. Their blackened ruins were to be a feature of the Irish landscape for many years afterwards.

By the spring of 1923, the anti-treaty IRA were finding it difficult to continue their campaign. The Southern Division of the IRA informed the IRA chief of staff, Liam Lynch, that, 'In a short time we would not have a man left owing to the great number of arrests and casualties.' Lynch, however, was determined to continue the armed struggle.

It was at this stage, in the last weeks of the Irish Civil War, that the violence reached a peak. March 1923 was described by Republicans in Kerry as, 'The terror month'. The most notorious event was the Ballyseedy Massacre. In revenge for the death of five Free State soldiers who had been killed by a booby-trap bomb, nine Republican prisoners were taken to the Ballyseedy crossroads from the barracks where they had been held. Here, they were tied to a landmine which was then detonated. Amazingly, one of the prisoners, Stephen Fuller, survived when he was blown into a nearby field. In the 1930s, in his application for a military service pension, Fuller was described as 'a complete and permanent invalid'. The Ballyseedy Massacre, an event which left behind it a long legacy of accusation and incrimination in Irish history, was followed by a spiral of violence and counter-violence on both sides.

The violence was only ended when, on 10 April, the IRA chief of staff, Liam Lynch, was killed in action whilst fleeing from Nationalist forces. On 30 April 1923, his successor, Frank Aiken, urged by de Valera, called a ceasefire. On 24 May, he ordered his fighters to 'dump arms' and return home. The Irish Civil War had ended. No surrender was made and no formal end to the war was ever negotiated.

The pro-treaty party Cumann na nGaedheal (which became the parent party for Fine Gael in 1933) initially controlled parliament and began the task of rebuilding Ireland. The wounds of civil war lay unhealed. Some 12,000 anti-treaty Republicans were still in gaol, with 8,000 of them going on hunger strike in November 1923. The divisions only moved to the political arena once those who had opposed the Anglo-Irish Treaty were able to enter parliament in 1927.

It was de Valera who realized that a political solution was the only way forward to achieve full independence. In 1926 he founded the Fianna Fail party, which replaced Sinn Fein as the main Republican Party. Fianna Fail entered parliament in 1927 and, in 1932, they came to power in Ireland. De Valera went

Eamon de Valera, first Taoiseach of the Republic of Ireland and leader of Fianna Fail

on to dominate Irish politics for many decades to come. As leader of Fianna Fail he was head of government three times between 1932 and 1959. In 1937 he became the first Taoiseach (Prime Minister) of the Republic under the new constitution. In 1959 he resigned in order to become the President of Ireland, a post that he held until 1973. At the age of 90, when he finally retired from Irish politics, de Valera was the oldest head of state in the world.

It was through parliament that the anti-treaty republicans finally achieved their aims. What they could not achieve by violence, they did so through a series of acts of parliament. By 1939 they had managed to remove most of the 'objectionable' terms of the Anglo-Irish Treaty. A new constitution was set in place which asserted Irish sovereignty and included a new name, Eire. At the time, it still asserted this sovereignty over all of Ireland, including Ulster.

The Irish Republic had finally gained the independence that many had sought since 1801 but at great cost. The wounds that the period 1918 to 1923 left behind continue to shape Irish history.

CHAPTER 10
The emergence of modern Britain: economy, class and culture

IN MANY ASPECTS, SUCH AS POLITICS, SEXUAL liberation, class and culture, Britain after 1918 was a very different nation from the one that existed before 1914.

Britain became a more democratic society. All men and, in stages, women over 21 gained the parliamentary vote. The Representation of the People Act 1918 trebled the franchise from 7.7 million voters to 21.4 million. The political landscape was further changed by the split within and collapse of the Liberals as a party of government. The Labour Party had emerged from the war as the main alternative to the Conservatives, confirmed by the first ever Labour led government of Ramsay MacDonald in January 1924.

Society was also undergoing significant changes in the aftermath of war. The hierarchies and divisions of pre-war society were undergoing aspects of social levelling. The influence of the traditional landed upper classes was weakened by the increased taxation begun by the Liberals before 1914 and by a shift in power towards the business and industrial leaders who had prospered in the war. A visible sign of their demise was the closure of more and more of the great country houses after 1918. Increasing numbers worked in the professions and in the Civil Service, swelling the numbers of the middle classes. The balance within the working class also changed as more skilled employees were needed. It was, in addition, a more politically aware and powerful working class with the granting of the vote, the rise of Labour and a well-organized trade union movement.

Along with these social changes, many contemporaries commented on the weakening of social deference compared to before the war. The working classes were less willing to automatically give way to the middle and upper classes. A major factor in this was the experience of the soldiers in the trenches. One account by an American visitor to Britain in 1920 conveyed the concern that his old friend in Oxford felt about the weakening of the class idea in post-war Britain. 'Ten years ago', described his friend, 'when I got onto a crowded bus, a working man would rise and touch his cap and give me his seat. I am sorry to see that spirit dying out'. A generation of young men had been changed by their wartime experiences. Rewarded with the vote and more politically aware, many were less willing to accept the established social order.

The world of the landed aristocracy was going through a period of important change after 1918, a change that was not confined to the weakening of social hierarchy. Many of their great houses were also beginning to disappear.

The period of Edwardian England before World War 1 had, in many ways, been the high point of a privileged and sheltered way of life for the aristocracy. Many of the great families had still retained their ancestral family homes spread around the counties. The pre-war years were the high point of the country house, with lavish house parties catered for by an array of servants and staff. The great houses were not only places to live and to entertain. They were the powerhouses of aristocratic influence in the counties. The local landed families were major employers and suppliers of housing to their workers. They were dominant figures in the social life of the county and often in local politics, although this had been weakened by the development of county councils in the late 19th century. Much of this traditional lifestyle and influence was to be swept away by the impact and aftermath of WW1. In some areas of rural Britain the loss of the 'big house' was tantamount to a social revolution.

The removal of the country houses did not begin in 1918. There had always been a tradition of knocking down and rebuilding in a more modern style. Think only of the replacement of mediaeval houses with the latest Elizabethan style in the 16th century, many of which were themselves replaced by new buildings in the Restoration period of the late 17th century or in the Georgian and Victorian eras of the 18th and 19th centuries. What was different from 1918 onwards, however, is that increasing numbers of great houses were pulled down and not rebuilt. Where the buildings survived, it was often with new, non-aristocratic owners, or they were put to different uses such as schools.

The war itself was a major catalyst for change.

The country houses had always been labour intensive, relying on an army of domestic servants and staff to manage the estate. Many workers left to serve in the armed forces during the war or were drawn to better paid jobs in munitions and other factories. Once they had tasted freedom from the strictly regulated country house lifestyle and benefited from better pay elsewhere, many were reluctant to return.

The period before 1914 had also seen the beginning of a changed attitude towards taxing the wealthy landed aristocracy. This was linked to the beginnings of the welfare state under the Liberals from 1906 onwards. In 1907 Asquith had introduced a tax that was more punitive for those whose income came from investments rather than earned income. This hit directly on the gentry and

Conservative poster from the 1909 election

aristocracy with their inherited wealth. Then, in 1909, Lloyd George introduced his People's Budget.

This was fiercely resisted by the aristocracy in the House of Lords before being forced through by the Parliament Act 1911. Henceforth, the super-rich were to face greatly increased scales of taxation. The costs of waging war forced the government to raise levels of taxation even further. The overall burden of direct taxation on the country estates rose from an average of 9% of income before WW1 to an average of 30% after it. The Earl of Pembroke's Wilton estate, for example, was paying 25% of its estate revenues on income tax in 1919 compared to 4% in 1914.

The war also saw the death of many male heirs to the great estates, especially given the high death rate among officers in the trenches. This weakened the landed estates in different ways. In some cases, there was simply nobody left to inherit. In others, the estate was subject to crippling death duties. Some families had tried to avoid death duties by giving their properties to their heirs. If the heir then died in battle, no death duty was levied. If, however, the heir was single and had no child to succeed, as was the case with many young men, the estate reverted back to the former owner. It would, once again, become subject to death duty.

Thirkleby Hall, near Thirsk, was one such estate that was sold off in 1919 as a direct result of the death of the heir during WW1. It had been the home of the Frankland family since the early 17th century. The estate was sold in 1919 and the house demolished in 1927. Today it is the site of a caravan park.

Crippled by income tax, by death duties or the loss of an heir, by the problems of finding staff and by lower farm incomes after 1918, many of the aristocratic families were forced to adapt to the changing times. Not even the great families were completely sheltered from the financial pressures of the post-war era, forced to sell possessions or to reduce the size of their estates. Miranda Carter, *The Great Silence 1918-20. Living in the Shadow of the Great War* describes the Duke of Devonshire presiding miserably over the demolition of the great conservatory at Chatsworth and having to sell off his London home to pay death duties. Many chose to demolish the great house which had become an unsustainable drain on their resources. Others sold some or even all of the estate itself. Where a family owned more than one estate, as many of the great families did, then they would often sell the least attractive or profitable. The Duke of Northumberland, for example, sold Stanwick Park in Yorkshire in 1918 to pay death duties. The family retained Alnwick Castle in Northumberland as their main family seat. In some cases the estate was bought for other uses, such as schools or country hotels. Where the estate was bought as a going concern, the buyers were often

Hamilton Palace, the seat of the Dukes of Hamilton, built in 1695 and demolished in 1921. (WW1 postcard)

wealthy businessmen who had profited from the war to make a fortune.

The ending of the war brought a period of social and economic unrest. At the heart of the unrest were issues that are still relevant today, such as the role of government, fiscal policy and Britain's economy in a changing world.

Pre-WW1 had been an era of major industrial unrest, led by the triple alliance of miners, railway men and transport workers. Thirty-eight million days were lost to strike action in 1912. There was a marked decrease in industrial unrest after 1914. The Munitions of War Act of July 1915 had bound unions involved in war work not to strike. In return, workers gained benefits from increased government control, such as national wage levels. The coming of peace, however, brought a return to economic and social instability. The ending of government controls and the move back towards privatization, combined with the post-war slump in the economy, brought renewed clashes between the trade union movement, government and employers. In 1919 more British workers were involved in strikes than in Germany. The unrest was epitomized in the Battle of George Square when protestors against wage cuts in Glasgow battled with police.

During WW1 Britain had incurred debts equivalent to 136% of its gross national product. Although demobilization did take place without major problems, there was certain to be an increase in unemployment. Wartime industries such as munitions, coal mining, ship building and iron began to contract. Countries such as the USA and Japan had taken over some of Britain's pre-war markets. Exports stood at 75% of their pre–war levels. It is also argued that British industry suffered from being the first country to industrialize such that, by 1918, it was suffering from structural weaknesses in its inability to cope with a changing world. By 1921 unemployment stood at 11.3%, the highest level since records began in 1881.

At the heart of the unrest was a debate about the role of government. World War 1 had greatly increased the role of government. This had been justified by the Defence of the Realm Act (DORA), first introduced in 1914. By 1918, political ideology had entered the realm of wartime policy. Clause IV of the new Labour constitution, drawn up in 1918, called for public ownership of the means of production, that is to say, the nationalization of industry. In the background was the Communist Revolution of November 1917, as a result of which Russia had abolished private ownership of industry.

In this charged atmosphere, the Coalition Government of Lloyd George had to try and balance political and social demands, both from the upper and from the lower classes,

George Square riots, Glasgow 1919

with the economic and fiscal constraints of wartime debt and post-war depression.

The sacrifices of WW1, the first total war, had led to Lloyd George's promise to create 'a land fit for heroes to live in'. In February 1918 an ambitious reform programme had been drawn up by the Minister of Reconstruction, Dr Christopher Addison. At its heart was a Housing Act that promised 500,000 houses within three years. 'Homes for Heroes'. This was an important landmark. For the first time in Britain, housing was made a national responsibility and the task to ensure that houses were built was handed to local authorities, hence the term 'council houses'. This alone was an important development in the provision of housing in the 20th century.

Council houses built in the 1920s

Under the pressure of post-war recession, the promise to create a 'land fit for heroes' came under severe pressure.

In response to the economic and financial pressures facing Britain at the end of the war, the Cunliffe Committee (1919) recommended a return to the stability of the gold standard at its pre-war level. This could only be achieved by a severe deflation of wages and prices in order to 'balance the budget'. To 'balance the budget' became the main aim of the Conservative majority in the coalition government, a policy that they pursued at a time of severe economic recession. What followed were swingeing cuts in public spending to balance the books and to ward off inflation. The cuts were termed the Geddes Axe, after Eric Geddes, Chair of the Committee on National Expenditure. It recommended major cuts in housing, education, welfare and defence. £30 million was cut from social services alone during 1922-3. Only 213,000 of the promised 500,000 council houses were built in the post-war period.

In a manner which bears parallels with the present day crisis, public debt as a % of GDP continued to rise, despite (or because of) severe deflation, reaching 1.76% by 1923.

As the government struggled with social welfare and fiscal economies, so the ending of the war also brought a return to industrial unrest. At its heart was the clash between private enterprise, government intervention and the demands of labour, represented through their trade unions and enforced by strike action.

The revival of industrial unrest in 1918 centred on the miners. Mining before 1914 had been fragmented and highly inefficient, with over 3,000 mines owned by 1,500 firms. In 1917 Lloyd George's Coalition Government had taken control over the mining industry for the duration of the war. In 1918, with the return of peace, the owners were anxious to regain control. They expected price rises as markets re-opened after the war. The miners, in contrast, were not keen to lose their wartime advantages, such as a national wage rate. The government set up the Sankey Commission in 1918. Sankey recommended the setting up a Ministry of Mining and complete state ownership of the mining industry. Lloyd George, however, was not support-ive of full state control being made permanent. Then, in 1920-21, coal exports and the price obtained for coal fell sharply. By 1921 losses per ton on coal averaged 5s (25p) or £5m a month across the industry. The government announced that it was going to hand back ownership to the mine owners when the present agreement finished at the end of March. The owners immediately gave notice that wages would have to be reduced because of lower coal prices. Wages in 1921 were at their inter-war peak of 88s 9d (£4.44p) a week. The mine owners wanted large reduc-tions, as much as 49% in the less profitable pits. On 1 April

Striking Wigan miners

199

1921 the miners were locked out. A week later the triple alliance called for a national strike, to begin on 15 April.

The context was not encouraging. By the summer of 1921, two million were unemployed. J. H. Thomas, the railway workers leader, and A. Bevin, the transport workers' leader, were more cautious than Frank Hodges, the miners' leader. The government was determined not to give in to the unions. Lloyd George called up 80,000 special constables and even placed machine guns at some pitheads. Public opinion was fanned with stories of gangs of miners terrifying the safety teams on the pumps. Even during a strike the mines had to be pumped of water or they risked never being worked again. This government propaganda was simply not true. Safety men worked as normal. The government insisted that the miners were, 'Resolved to let the mines go to destruction in the belief that they will intimidate the government into surrender to their demands. The nation is for the first time confronted by an attempt to coerce it into capitulation by the destruction of its resources.' Despite government rhetoric, public opinion was broadly sympathetic to the miners as they learned more about the proposed wage cuts. Even the Minister of Labour stated that, 'A drop from 88s to 44s is a bit thick.'

Lloyd George turned the stand-off into a political issue. Hodges' main demand was that a national wage needed to be ensured by pooling profits from the more profitable mines to support those which were less profitable. Lloyd George said that this was only possible to enforce if the government nationalized the mines. He said that Hodges was pursuing a political aim by trying to force the government to adopt a socialist policy. This same constitutional issue was to be the basis of government resistance in the General Strike of 1926. At the last minute, Lloyd George was able to exploit negotiating differences between Hodges, the majority of his own union, and the other two unions. The railway men and the transport workers pulled back from a general strike. The miners were left to go it alone. They stayed out for three months before being forced back to work by the owners, with greatly reduced wages and no national wage level. The average weekly wage dropped from 88s 9d (£4.44p) to 58s 10d (£2.99p).

The collapse of the triple alliance in April 1921 was termed Black Friday in the history of the trade union movement but the struggle was not over. In 1925 the mine owners gave notice that they would return to an eight hour day and further reduce wages. The miners responded with the cry, 'Not a penny off the pay, not a second on the day.' The result was the General Strike of 4 to 11 May 1926 with a large percentage of organized labour coming out in sympathy for the miners. It proved a failure, although the miners stayed on strike until November 1926. The failure began a reduction in the number of mines and an exodus of miners from the coalfields, a decline portrayed in novels such as George Orwell's *The Road to Wigan Pier* (1937). It is a decline that was to continue throughout the 20th century to the present day.

Women's jobs and expectations were central to this period of economic instability and a changing labour market.

Views about gender imbalances caused by the war differ. Vera Britten *Testament of Youth* (1933) wrote of the 'lost generation' of young women as a result of more than 700,000 British male casualties in the war which deprived the interwar generation of husbands. The Daily Mail wrote about 'our surplus girls'. Martin Pugh *Wish You Were Here? Britain between the Wars*, argues against over-exaggeration. He points out that, in fact, marriage rates post-1918 picked up quickly because the losses and instability of war encouraged more people to marry. The figures are open to interpretation. Of the 1.75 million unmarried women documented in the early 1920s, half were still unmarried 10 years later. In 1919, the government established the Society for the Overseas Settlement of British Women. The next year, 125,000 women did emigrate, mostly to the dominions, though their marriage prospects were not necessarily improved by emigration given the mortality rates among young men from the Empire who had fought in World War 1.

The era after WW1 was a complex one for young women. Many felt 'Let out of the cage' by the experiences and greater freedom given to them by the war. The 1918 Reform Act, however, failed to extend the vote to the majority of these women when it set the female franchise at an age of 30. The government had no desire to create a majority of women voters, which it would have done if women had been given the same voting rights as men. At the same time, women were being pressured to give up their wartime jobs, where they still existed, to the returning soldiers.

Marriage remained the expected norm for women, who were still pressured into giving up their jobs when they did marry. This was despite the gender imbalance after the war. Isobel Passey of Woolwich wrote in the Daily Herald in October 1919 that, 'No decent man would allow his wife to work.' This attitude and expectation became formalized by marriage bars in the civil service, teaching and nursing, which meant that women were expected to give up their jobs once they married. Many other companies and professions had unofficial bars. This was despite the Sex Disqualification (Removal) Act passed in 1919, which was meant to ensure that women were not discriminated against simply because of their gender. The 1921 census showed that there was a lower percentage of women working than there had been in 1911. Despite the effects of the war and the liberation of women that it brought, Britain was still a society where middle class women would automatically stay at home once they married and changed their dress after lunch to receive visitors.

Despite the efforts and wishes of the traditional establishment to turn the clock back to 1914, however, society was in a process of change.

Society had a different 'feel' to it compared to before 1914, particularly among the younger generation. People were keen to enjoy themselves after the privations of war. This was especially so with the children of the upper and middle classes, dubbed 'Bright Young Things'. What began as elaborate treasure hunts around London, developed into a hedonistic lifestyle of drink, drugs and jazz clubs. Changes in appearance and lifestyle were not, however, confined to the affluent. The term 'Flapper' was used as early as 1918 in a *Times* article to refer to an independent young woman. The appearance of these young women was beginning to change, influenced by a rejection of constraining pre-war fashion and by the styles of Coco Chanel, the first woman to wear trousers, cut her hair to a bob and reject the corset. It was in 1920 that Coco Chanel introduced her chemise, a simple, short, loose dress. The Flapper look, with lighter materials and shorter length skirts, allowed young women to literally kick up their heels when doing the new dances such as the Charleston.

A group of flappers from the mid-1920s

It may have been a reaction to the loss of so many lives in the Great War. Certainly there was also the influence of American culture on the younger generation. Jazz was seen as modern. By 1925 11,000 night clubs were operating in London. This new culture was a challenge to the older generation and a visible sign of change. The Charleston was denounced in the *Daily Mail* 1922 as, 'Reminiscent only of Negro dances'.

Women had greater freedom outside marriage and more control over their bodies within marriage thanks to Marie Stopes and changing attitudes towards contraception. One aspect of marriage that did change in the early 1920s was a lowering of family sizes compared to the Victorians. The average for married women in the 1890s was just over four children. By the 1930s this had fallen to just over two. Britain was moving towards the modern nuclear family.

As the British government and economy, especially its traditional Victorian economy which was based on heavy industry, was struggling to respond and adapt to the post-war world, so the shoots of a new, more modern Britain were starting to take hold. This was especially so in London and the south-east. In central London, new office jobs were being created for a new generation of corporations and banking. ICI and British Petroleum both opened large head offices in central London. Factories were being built along the main arterial roads, such as the Firestone Tyre Factory on the Great West Road and Wrigley's at Wimbledon. They were typical of a new generation of London's light industry, based in modern buildings and using electrically-powered machinery.

Willys Overland Crossley factory

These new light industries and office work offered new employment opportunities to women in the 1920s. Work as a typist, it was said, could transport a woman into the middle classes. Access was, however, not always equal in Britain at this time. In the industrial north, family tradition often still determined destination. 'I was born a lace worker', a Nottingham woman explained. There could also be social restrictions that we can hardly imagine today. Having separated parents might, for example, bar a young woman from gaining respectable shop work.

Aspirations and models were, however, changing. Even mill girls with means, it was said, dressed like typists.

The writer J.B. Priestley gave a description of this changing England in his work, *English Journey*, written some ten years later in 1934. There still existed, he wrote, '... the nineteenth-century England, the industrial England of coal, iron, steel, cotton, wool, railways ... This England makes up the larger part of the Midlands and the North'.

Then he described the, '... new post-war England. America, I suppose was its real birthplace. This is the England of by-pass roads, of filling stations, giant cinemas, bungalows with tiny garages, factory girls looking like actresses'.

A new England was emerging after the Great War. In the period 1918 to 1924 its development was still limited by geography, by generation and, in some cases, by gender. There was still much that was traditional and would have been recognizable to a pre-war generation. Change was, however, taking place. Modern Britain was beginning to take shape in the period after World War 1, a Britain that would have been more recognizable to us today than the one that existed before 1914.